DEAR THOMAS

BY DANYELLE CEDAR

A MEMOIR

Published by Savage Press

ISBN: 979-8-9879338-0-0 / Hardcover Edition
ISBN: 979-8-9879338-1-7 / Paperback Edition
ISBN: 979-8-9879338-2-4 / eBook Edition

Growing up, you are told to stay away from drugs. You are told why they are bad. What you are never told is the hell you will go through loving someone who is addicted to drugs.

You are never given a textbook about addiction, and never given homework on how to handle manipulation and lies. You are never quizzed how to slow the anxiety, how to go with gut instinct, or how to not obsess over what they are doing at all times.

It is never explained that you will become a slave to the addict, a detective, a babysitter who has to know their location at all times—what they are doing, who they are with. It is never explained that even if they get through recovery, they are never cured of their addiction; they come back and haunt, turning your perfect world upside-down.

You are never told what to do when you realize they will never be their true selves again. You are never told what it will feel like when your heart is ripped in half, or the twist in your stomach when finding another needle, or that you will continue to give the addict the benefit of the doubt. Even when they are with you, you will grieve like they are dead.

It is never explained there is nothing more you can do for them, that ultimatums do not work, and that breaking the addiction has to be their choice.

It is never explained, even after three or four rehabs, that they may use again.

You are never told how hard it will be when you finally decide to walk away. You are never told how many tears you will cry when you force yourself to stop enabling, even if it means they are homeless, even if it means it's the last time you may ever see them alive.

You are never told about the fears rushing in your head over their safety after you have walked away. You are never told how you will scare yourself wondering if they owe someone money who might come after you for revenge.

Growing up, you are told to stay away from drugs and why they are bad, but you are never told even if you never try a drug in your life, they can kill you.

DEAR THOMAS

Dear Thomas,

My parents didn't know what the fuck they were doing. They had me at twenty-one. I wouldn't say they were *bad* parents, yet they were shitty roommates. There was always a roof over my head, a bed to sleep in, and food on the table, but aren't those prerequisites of being a parent?

I'm not ignorant. I know I was spoiled to grow up in Morro Bay, California. The beach was across the street, and there was a swing in the backyard, along with plenty of bikes and skateboards in the driveway. There were also a lot of late-night parties.

Morro Bay is a drinking town with a fishing problem. Growing up near the ocean with old plumbing, we were conditioned to never drink the tap water. One time I came out from my room when I was thirsty, after one of the late-parties went quiet. I couldn't find a single water bottle or juice box in the house, just towers of empty beer cans, and vodka and whiskey bottles spread across the kitchen counter. I started looking in every cup I could find, searching for water. I finally found a cup with clear liquid and chugged it. Not water. *Vodka.* I thought I was going to die. It was the most awful thing I had ever tasted at ten years old, worse than sour milk. I immediately spit it out and started crying.

Where are my parents? Where did everyone go?

I had no choice but to pour myself a glass of tap water from the bathroom sink. I couldn't stop crying, partly because I knew it was going to taste gross and partly because I knew I was going to be in trouble the next day when my dad found out.

Dear Thomas,

My dad managed a liquor store, which appropriately supported his party lifestyle. He made sure the house I grew up in was an elevated version of the home *he* grew up in: loud, chaotic, cussing, burping, wrestling, and broken furniture. There was a skateboard halfpipe next to my sandbox. Early on, I decided I wanted to be nothing like the people who raised me.

The intoxicated lifestyle was ugly and unattractive. This lifestyle was unfamiliar to my mom and she didn't know how to handle the chaos. The household *she* grew up in was quiet and "proper." Everything about my mom's upbringing was based on "saving face." The only dysfunction that existed in her home was the constant brushing of shit under the rug and living in denial that there was bad in the world.

As I got older, and our family grew, my dad's responsibilities expanded. He was always angry, tired, broke, and drunk. A control freak. He was obsessive, jealous, physically and verbally abusive. Nothing and no one was ever good enough. He would put anyone and everyone down to feel better about himself. He also made sure we would never be more successful than him in life. He shut my sister down when she wanted to play water polo because *he* didn't know how to play water polo. He chose to not finish college, so he shut down my dream of going to San Diego University. My mom wanted to quit her corporate job and become a massage therapist. To him, the idea of her touching a bare body was ludicrous.

My dad's high school sweetheart cheated on him, and her unplanned pregnancy was the physical evidence. My entire life, he cried about his ex-girlfriend, how she broke his heart and ruined him. He blamed his alcoholism and anger on her. I grew up hating this woman because supposedly she was the one to blame for all the abuse I endured. I would lay in bed and roll my eyes, thinking about his broken heart: *Get the fuck over it. It's been how many years?* And I would hurt for my mom. Was he not in love with her? If he was, why was he still hung up on this woman from high school?

I begged my mom at an early age to take us and leave my dad behind. I would sit at home and pray he'd die in a car accident and never come home again. My mom didn't have the strength to leave. She didn't think she could financially raise her kids alone. She would be embarrassed if her marriage failed, caught up in the bullshit American dream—dog behind a white picket fence, car in the driveway. It's ironic we never took a family portrait to hang on the wall.

I hardly saw my mom. She would leave for work before I woke for school and would come home after I went to bed. She lived in constant denial and had no desire to be home. She paid the bills while my dad ran the show. As the oldest, I got the brunt of everything. I took on the most abuse and responsibilities. I grew up faster than any of my friends.

I was sixteen when my dad checked himself into rehab to "save" his family. He was only sober for three months, long enough to rearrange his complicated life to convince my mom he was a changed man. He didn't give a shit about any of us. We weren't worth his sobriety.

A few months before my 18th birthday, I started looking for apartments. This inspired my mom to move out on her own, without telling me. She and my sister packed what they wanted, left a bunch of other shit, and abandoned me with my dad. I had begged her to leave this asshole ten years prior, but she waited until then to move out. She knew she wouldn't be able to survive living with her husband without me.

Dear Thomas,

I related more with the rebel crowd—the kids from broken homes—but I couldn't fuck off in the park like the rest. I had responsibilities. My best friends walked a straight line, but it was hard to relate when the grass in my backyard wasn't as green as theirs. My best friends did not share in the abuse I experienced at home.

At fourteen, I started sneaking out to attend high school parties. I was a social butterfly, but it never crossed my mind to cave into the peer pressure to drink alcohol, smoke weed, or snort cocaine. I have never had a desire to do anything just because everyone else was doing it.

I never wanted to drink alcohol. I was already too much like my dad. I get my hustle, sarcasm, sense of humor, and temper from him. Why the fuck would I want to be an alcoholic and turn ugly on the inside, like him? Alcoholism can be hereditary, and I don't ever want to find out if I have the same disease as my father.

There is nothing more annoying and judgmental than a jaw dropping when someone hears that I do not drink alcohol. Their lives come to a halt, insisting that I spill the *ME! True Hollywood Story*. What do they want to hear, that I'm an alcoholic and killed an innocent person while driving under the influence? That I was taken advantage of when incoherent? That I'm religious? These are all bullshit reasons for me not to drink.

"I choose not to drink alcohol" is never a good enough answer. It took me a long time to come up with "It's not my style" instead. That usually confuses people enough to not ask further questions. It's not the answer most expect.

Sometimes the insecure will argue, "But having drunk sex is *so* much fun!" Well, I fucking love sex, so much that I want to remember how amazing it was the next day, replaying it on a loop in my mind.

I have had boyfriends who felt uncomfortable drinking while in a relationship with me. I have never told anyone they weren't allowed alcohol if they wanted to be in a relationship with me. If any ex begs to differ, they were most likely insecure in our relationship and I'm glad they are somebody I *used* to know.

"Are you uncomfortable if I drink in front of you?"

"No. Are you uncomfortable if I *don't* drink in front of you?"

I can have a good time sober.

Not everyone is that secure with themselves.

Finding friends who accept me for me has always been a struggle. I could be at dinner and a friend would say, "You can't even taste the alcohol in this drink," which I find offensive. I don't give a fuck if you can or can't taste the alcohol. Who drinks for the taste? People consume because they want a change in their mind and body.

"I would love to see you drunk one day," some have said to me.

Why? What do they want to see: me throwing up over the toilet bowl, me unable to stand, me driving into a telephone pole? I can do those things sober.

If seeing me intoxicated is on someone's bucket list, their life is lame as fuck.

May 28, 2012

Dear Thomas,

Two things my mom and I have never done: taken a mother-daughter vacation or been to Hawaiʻi. We have always wanted to go to Hawaiʻi but couldn't afford it. My dad spent every spare dollar on alcohol while my mom spent every spare dollar on home renovations.

Now we can say we've done both. My mom and I spent last week in Maui. It was the best vacation I have ever experienced. Drama-free and full of adventure. I owe it all to her. She paid for and planned everything.

We snorkeled at Molokini, attended the Old Lāhainā Luau, ate at Mama's Fish House, went cliff jumping, and hiked through a majestic bamboo forest in Hāna. As we were hiking through the bamboo forest, there were smushed guavas all over the ground. The smell of fermented fruit reminded me of my childhood: stale beer cans my dad and uncles would pile up on the side of the house next to the trash bins.

We cruised down Front Street in Lāhainā. It reminded me of the Embarcadero in Morro Bay. I have absolutely fallen in love with Maui. Yesterday was our last full day and all I can think about is how I don't want to leave. I envy the simple life in Lāhainā. Everyone is friendly, laid-back, and have zero regrets for escaping the mainland rat race.

While floating on a paddle board and staring out at the ocean, I asked myself, "Could I move here? Would I be okay leaving everything I am familiar with, leaving everyone I know, and living on an island where I don't know anyone?"

The answer is yes.

I would leave everything to move to paradise.

Dear Thomas,

I turned twenty-one last month, and since I don't drink alcohol I decided to do something more memorable than bar-hopping: my mom and I went skydiving.

Also, I decided to move to Maui.

I spent the last six months working, saving money, and spending as much time as I could with friends and family. I sold my car and have been preparing for my move all week. My mom dropped me off at the airport at five this morning. This is the first time I have flown alone. The plane was full, except for one empty seat next to me, so I curled up into a ball across my two seats and slept the entire flight. As we prepared for landing, I was mesmerized by the turquoise water and the ability to see the ocean floor. And then it hit me: this was my new home.

I reached my destination this afternoon at the Shark Pit compound. The property owner showed me to my room, and later I met my roommates on the beach in front of the house for a New Year's Eve barbeque.

One of them asked, "Do you have a resolution?"

I shook my head no.

"I don't need one. I just moved to Maui."

February 1, 2015

Dear Thomas,

My boyfriend Brad quit drinking and wanted to get into freediving, and he's the reason I met you. Brad was dropping me off at work but picked you up along the way because you were going diving together. He was excited to have found you as a sober companion and freediving partner. Brad introduced us and shared that I also choose to be sober, and your response was, "I quit because I am absolutely stupid when I drink." That was almost two years ago.

It's been six months since I dumped that entitled, selfish, whiny little prick, and I am glad to be rid of that relationship. Since I left him, you and I don't cross paths or bump into each other anywhere in town. I liked being around you, especially when the two of you would go diving and you'd come to our apartment and cook the fish you caught.

I recently had a dream that you and I hooked up. I woke up wondering, *What was that?* Does my subconscious have you on my mind? How is it possible to have a dream about someone's body when you've never seen them naked in your bed. The human imagination is unreal. I told my roommate about it. She laughed and said, "Brad would freak out if you guys got together." *No shit.*

I went to a concert last night. I don't know how this conversation started with a group of friends, but we decided that men who are "ass guys" are good, whereas men who are "boob guys" are douchebags. We sat in the grass and texted every guy in our phones.

"I'm taking a poll. Boobs or ass? Pick only one."

You texted back immediately: ass.

Exactly what I wanted to confirm.

March 11, 2015

Dear Thomas,

I had another dream about us being together. What does it mean? I wish I could organically bump into you somewhere, like the grocery store or beach. I get butterflies every time you like one of my photos on Instagram. I can't stop thinking about you, and I wonder what it would be like if we dated.

"Hey, do you ever want to hang out?" I finally texted.

Forty-five minutes later: "Yeah, sure, that sounds good :) I'm down."

You invited me kayaking but I had to work. You invited me hiking but it rained. But then on an overcast morning you finally came over to watch a movie. It was nice to catch up since we hadn't seen each other in a while. We talked about our favorite movies, music, and hobbies. We made fun of tourists, talked about work, goals, and our aspirations in life.

You revealed to me that you recently had surgery for a deviated septum that hindered your freediving potential, and that you were nervous about the aftercare medication because of your history with drug use.

"I could never imagine you *not* sober."

"I was the worst person you could ever know."

"I can't imagine that."

You left when I had to get ready for work, but it was a nice ice-breaker for us, and I kept wondering when we could get together again to maybe "Netflix and Chill." I guess you were wondering the same because you sent a text: "We need to try that again :)"

I was blushing when I replied, "Definitely."

"What time are you off tonight?"

"I usually get home around eleven."

"My place or yours?"

"Doesn't matter."

"Let's do my place :)"

It was easy to keep a smile on my face my entire shift. I arrived at your house close to midnight. We started watching a movie until we wanted to "Chill."

Dear Thomas,

I have enjoyed our adult slumber parties these past five months. I'd like to hang out with you outside the bedroom more often, but we have both been busy working.

Over the summer, you helped me get my first credit card. Thank you for helping me get to this next level of adulthood. You showed me where I could apply, and my plastic $300-limit arrived in the mail. And just before your birthday you got your driver's license back after not having it for almost ten years. You saved up and bought a new Toyota Tacoma, then called me because you were excited to pick me up so we could break in the backseat.

Three nights ago, I suggested we go to the movies. You had gotten off work early because of an injury and texted me a selfie rocking a new eyepatch the doctors had taped to your eye while waiting in the emergency room.

"What happened?"

"I was grinding metal and fragments got in."

"No safety goggles?"

"Yeah, but they still got in somehow."

I texted each night to make sure you were feeling okay since you were uncomfortable and not sleeping. It's extra hot this summer and you don't have air conditioning, which makes sleeping even more uncomfortable. I have air conditioning in my living room, and offered to move my mattress to sleep in there a few nights.

"Fuck, I can't sleep," you texted one night. "My eye is driving me nuts. Do you know someone who might have an extra pain pill or something?"

I offered ibuprofen and Excedrin, but you had already

tried both and it wasn't helping, so you were going to try NyQuil.

"You don't have a cold," I said.

"It might help me sleep. What I am really looking for is Vicodin."

This raised my eyebrows since you are a recovering addict. You have been sober for almost five years and I know you wouldn't jeopardize your sobriety. I assumed you knew what you could or couldn't handle. You must have been in a lot of pain. A friend of mine had Xanax. I don't even know what Xanax is, but apparently it could be used as a muscle relaxer. It was midnight when I drove to her house to get it for you.

I fell asleep next to you that night. I didn't wake you when I left in the morning, but I kissed you on the temple next to your bad eye.

Dear Thomas,

I invited you to my birthday party, but you had to work. You didn't even text until two days later: "How was your birthday, bubble butt?" I wish you could have been there or at least wished me a happy birthday. It was a lot of fun and you missed out.

Until last night, I hadn't seen you in over a month, and you're a lot skinnier. I spent two weeks in California for my brother's wedding. Since I got back, you and I have been missing each other because I work days and you have been working more graveyard shifts.

"I've been dieting and cutting weight for freediving," you said, even though I made you brownies and you were more than happy to break your diet.

I woke up in the middle of the night when you seemed like you were having a panic attack. You held your chest, making strange faces, and you were doing something with your lips like you were thirsty or had cotton-mouth.

"Are you okay?"

"I'm fine."

I wasn't going to pry, but after you left my *hānai* sister Piper said, "Dude, Thomas is on drugs. He kept me up all night because he was pacing in and out of the kitchen."

"There's no way Thomas is on drugs."

Dear Thomas,

Something's going on with you but I can't figure it out. I have always appreciated how you text me back right away, or within a couple hours if you are working, but I hadn't heard from you in over a week. Then you posted on Facebook, "Love everyone, see you soon!"

"Everything okay?" I texted, but you didn't respond for another week.

"I had to go to detox because I was using drugs again," you finally answered. "I just got out today and still feel a little crummy but I will be okay. Sorry for not letting you know. I feel much better and am never doing that shit again."

I sat in shock. Piper was right. You were using. What the fuck? I guess you needed a reminder of how awful using drugs feels.

I let you know I wanted to see you, but didn't want to bother you or stress you out while starting your twelve-step program all over again.

Your mom was in town and she was rightfully paranoid when you told her you were coming over to spend a couple hours with me. I have never met your mom before so you asked me to speak with her over the phone. I enjoyed talking to her and shooting the shit. She wanted to make sure you were safe and weren't lying when you said you were going to my house.

"I know my son and he is a liar."

That made me sad. I don't feel that way about you.

I was training for my concierge job when Piper texted:

"Where is Thomas going?"

"What do you mean?"

"Check his Facebook."

At the top of the page was a screenshot of your airline itinerary. MAUI > LAX > TEXAS. What is in Texas? *Who* is in Texas? You can't stand the mainland or the cold; and you are flying to Texas in the middle of December? It appeared to be a one-way ticket.

I texted Piper, safely assuming: "He is going to rehab."

December 20, 2015

Dear Thomas,

I sent one of your friends a message hoping to receive information about your stay in Texas. This friend confirmed you are in treatment and gave me the address so I could send you this letter. I hope you get it before Christmas.

When I first met you, I was stoked to meet someone sober because I don't come across enough of them. I don't know when I developed a crush on you because I was living with my boyfriend at the time, but I was always excited when I heard you were staying the night because you two would go diving in the morning. You were nice to look at and I cannot express enough how much I respected you for being sober. After I ended the relationship with my boyfriend, I didn't see you for maybe seven months. But I thought about how much I missed being around you. I don't know if you remember, but I couldn't hold it in anymore.

"Hey, do you ever want to hang out?"

And you know the rest of the story.

I miss you. I hope you are doing well. Please stay as long as you need to get healthy. I don't know when you'll be home or when I get to see you, but I will be so happy when I do.

Dear Thomas,

You have returned to Maui and I cannot wait to see you! I am looking forward to everything returning exactly the way it was before, hence the message:

"Can we start hanging out more outside the bedroom."

"I can't do relationships, they scare me."

What does that even mean?

I cannot stand it when people say relationships scare them. To me it's an excuse. It brings me back to listening to my dad talk about his broken heart.

I have heard from mutual friends that you had your heart broken badly by your high school love, Whitney. I have had my heart broken before too. It's not fun, but that was a long time ago. How long are you going to hold yourself back from being open to love?

Dear Thomas,

We've spent a few nights together since your return—the usual Netflix and Chill. I want a relationship with substance but I'll take whatever I can get with you. But tonight, when I asked if you wanted to come over after work, you changed everything.

"I can't see you anymore."

"What do you mean?"

"My sponsor said I cannot see you anymore. It's a rule that I cannot date or have sexual relations in my first year of recovery. Trust me, I fought him on this. But I have to do what I have to do to stay sober."

Those words hit me hard. I have so many questions, but I want nothing but the best for you. I only have good intentions. You are the company you keep, and I am sober!

When my godfather got sober after being arrested for a DUI, his wife would still have her vodka martinis in front of him. When my dad returned from rehab, my mom would still enjoy her glass of wine at dinner in front of him. I did not respect her for that. Her argument was that *she* didn't have a drinking problem. Drinking problem or not, it's rude, disrespectful, and unsupportive. Recovery is an uphill battle and requires support.

I recognize I will always come second after your recovery, but I can't help but take this personally. You must plan on being lonely for the rest of your life because you will never meet a woman like me. A woman who is sober and isn't an AA member. A woman who will love you and accept you for exactly the person you are. A woman who will drop everything for you in a second. A woman who believes in you the way I do. A woman as patient as me. A woman who is madly in love with you. Truly, madly, deeply in love with you.

I feel like my heart has been ripped out of my chest.

February 13, 2016

Dear Thomas,

While you were in rehab, I was hired to work at the Black Rock Resort. I didn't pick where I worked; I was assigned to this property, the same property where you work. You've been back for over a month and we haven't crossed paths because it is a large hotel. I stay in the lobby, and you mostly work behind the scenes, wherever maintenance is needed.

I'm still upset since you said you couldn't see me anymore. It hurts and I am selfishly mad that you relapsed in the first place. You were almost five years sober but you having to start over means forfeiting your "privilege" to date.

I was in the cafeteria on my lunch break when you walked past me. You froze, remembering I work here too. I couldn't even muster the word "hi."

My mind raced: *What the fuck. This is uncomfortable. I wish I could see you.* A couple minutes passed as you were making your plate and then you sat next to me. *To be nice? Shouldn't you be sitting at a different table?*

I mean, you won't date me and you can't have sex with me, and you would never agree to go out in public, so why did you sit next to me? Then chef Jim at the table asked if I had a Valentine's date.

"Nope."

I made sure you felt that. If I wanted someone to be my Valentine, it would be you. It's funny Jim asked me that in front of you, unaware of our history.

Soon after I went back to my desk, you walked through the lobby to light the tiki torches in the driveway and around the grounds. How is it I have now seen you twice in one shift?

Dear Thomas,

Now you don't go a single shift without making sure I notice you. When I'm at my desk, you come by to change light bulbs in the lobby, or say hello to the valet guys, or light the tiki torches. You also eat at the same time I do. You say you're not allowed to be with me, nor do you want to be in a relationship, but I can't help but believe you have feelings for me. If you didn't, you wouldn't make it a point to see me so often.

It is torturous to work around you. My coworker came up with a code word. Whoever spots you first, front desk agent or lobby concierge, they say, "Watermelon," warning me not to look up and give you the attention you're seeking.

"Watermelon," someone called.

I was cutting papers at my desk. You were in my peripheral, hitting the janitor keys clipped to your hip to make sure I could hear you.

How did it feel that you failed to make me look?

"Fuck, I don't want a girlfriend, but I want to fuck," you texted later.

Should I be flattered, or should I be insulted?

I don't have any desire to date anyone else on this island. I feel like I've been put in limbo. You can't have sexual relations for one year, so I'll wait a full year to be with you again. Maybe, by then, you will want to be in a relationship.

Dear Thomas,

A year ago your goal was to free dive over 200 feet. This month you set two new records for yourself. Breath hold: four minutes and six seconds. Deepest dive: 199 feet. These are both huge accomplishments! I would love for you to take me freediving.

You crushed my heart but assured me we could still be friends, but what does that even mean? You don't invite me to anything like you do with your other friends.

In a moment of weakness, I texted you how lonely I felt:

"Not being with you is extremely difficult. My heart hurts. Is it so much to want to cuddle and fall asleep in your arms? I should probably stop talking to you."

"We can still be friends. I don't want to lose you."

"Then meet me at the beach this weekend."

"Let's hang out sooner, like now."

Your text messages turned sloppy after that. I drove to your friend's house where you invited me to meet you, and texted you to come out as soon as I parked.

You grabbed me by the hips, lifted me against the side of the car, and started making out with me, but something didn't feel right. Where was this coming from? I broke away to say hello, but you wouldn't look directly into my eyes. You wouldn't look at me period.

"Thomas, have you been drinking?"

"Yes, I had some beer."

You relapsed, *again*.

Dear Thomas,

Two nights ago was one of the longest nights of my life. I knew you were drinking but I had no idea what drugs you were using before I arrived. You were the happiest I had ever seen you. We had wild sex, but I cannot be happy about you relapsing.

At one point you turned paranoid and ran out of the house completely naked. I don't know where you went, but I was freaking out because we didn't need the neighbors calling the cops and you being arrested for indecent exposure. I walked the neighborhood but couldn't find you. I came back inside and looked in the backyard and there you were, hugging bamboo.

Getting you to sleep was near impossible. I finally got you to fall asleep around four in the morning. I did not sleep at all, and I had to be at work by seven. Your previous relapse lasted four months, so I'm hopeful you're willing to go back to rehab soon.

When I got off work yesterday, you texted me to come back over for a repeat of the previous night. When I showed up, you were asleep. You woke up around sunset and started freaking out that you'd missed your shift at work, even though you told me it was your day off. How could you go to work in this condition? I watched you call your boss and apologize for missing your shift, then realized you thought it was the next morning already.

You thought we were watching the sunrise, but it was the sunset.

Your next shift didn't start for a couple hours, so you called back and let your boss know you could work. I found someone who provided you Suboxone to get you through your shift with as little anxiety as possible. You also asked me to get you a Hyrdo Flask full of kratom tea. Kratom is supposed to help with overcoming opioid withdrawals, but it's more like heroin brewed in a glass of hot water.

After you got home from your graveyard shift and went to sleep, it was my turn to work. When I finished my shift, I brought you a Subway sandwich and Copenhagen chew.

"I'm grateful for all the help this week," you said.

You paid me back for all the food, medication, chew, cigarettes, and beer as soon as you got paid. It's easy to help when you're a stand-up guy and pay me back so quickly.

Dear Thomas,

The past month's routine: I wake up early to go to work, bring you lunch and cigarettes, we fall asleep with the TV on, and then repeat it all over again.

At one point, you ran out of your antidepressant medication. Someone with the same prescription was kind enough to bring you a dose of theirs—not something they usually have to spare, or should spare—but you saw your doctor the next day for a refill.

You flew to the big island this week to stay with your parents in Kona. You had this week requested as vacation time months ago. There's an annual freediving competition you always go to and usually dominate, but this year you threw that away when you decided to drink again. You stopped training and were in no condition to dive.

I picked you up from the airport and could tell you were upset. Your dive buddies had been texting you asking why you weren't at the competition. They had all looked forward to seeing you, but I wouldn't doubt some were stoked they had a chance at winning. You have always been the free diver others aspire to be.

September 12, 2016

Dear Thomas,

I met your mom for the first time. Barbara is a hoot, to say the least. She's small but feisty as fuck. I like her a lot. She's loud, opinionated, and cusses a lot, like me.

She is a functional alcoholic herself. She knows how to get through a twelve-pack a day, but also works hard running her own cleaning business in Kona.

You love when your mom comes to Maui because she takes care of you. She fills your fridge with food and candy and booze. You fall asleep in her arms when she's watching *Law & Order*. And when she's not here, you have me to do all those same things for you. Barbara has figured out I am the only person she can trust on Maui who cares for your wellbeing.

"I will always be there for him," I told her.

She was here for three days but you didn't spend a moment with her. You lied and told her you were going to an AA meeting. Instead, you got high.

"This is why I don't do relationships," you said, "because I am a mess and I hurt everyone close to me."

Dear Thomas,

I have gone above and beyond taking care of you the past six weeks. Any night I thought I'd sleep at my own house, you'd text me things like, "Starting to have convulsions. I really need someone to be here. And need a beer, bad. Don't want to have a seizure."

One night, I parked my car in the complex and could hear you screaming from the parking lot. When you have convulsions, you have these awful screams that wake up the neighbors. You don't even realize you're screaming half the time. I ran up to the second floor of the building and bolted through your front door. You were burning up but sometimes it is hard to tell if you have a fever because it's so hot in Lāhainā. I pointed the fan in your direction, but you told me the fan gave you the chills while having alcohol withdrawals.

You couldn't stop shaking. I curled into bed with you and wrapped my arms and legs around you. I'm half your size but I was trying my best to help keep you from shaking. It took a few hours to get you to fall asleep. When I hold you, you don't scream.

Your mom texted me asking if I had spoken to you because you weren't answering her calls. I let her know I was there, holding you. Every night I sleep at your house is another night your mom sleeps a little better because she knows you're safe.

Ever since you were fired from your job your parents have been paying your rent. Your mom cannot fathom the thought of you being homeless. They also take care of your truck payments. I don't know why you still have the truck;

it's not like you have anywhere to be since you were fired from your job. Both you and your mom have interrupted many of my days at work. She doesn't trust you so she puts money in my bank account so I can write the check to your property manager, fill your gas tank, grocery shop for you, buy cigarettes, alcohol, and the rest of the insanity.

You text while I am in the middle my shift that you're starving or out of cigarettes, or that you need me. I cannot be bothered at work every fucking day because you're hungry and incapable of buying food over drugs.

As a concierge, certain activity companies gift me incentives when I book their services, usually in the form of grocery gift cards. I have given these to you to buy yourself food, but instead you used them as a form of payment to buy drugs, 'cause drug dealers gotta eat too. I gave those gift cards to you because it didn't feel like money out of my pocket. However, those *were* meals that never made it to my mouth. I earned those gift cards. Not you. Not your drug dealer.

Another day, you asked me to leave work on my lunch break to bring you kratom tea because you needed help detoxing. You wouldn't wait until I got off at three. You needed me to run to your rescue at *your* convenience. I left work to bring you what you needed. When I arrived, your bedsheets were disgusting. There was melted ice cream and cigarette burns in the sheets your mom just bought you. And somehow the Ben & Jerry's made it to the ceiling. What the fuck happened? Then I noticed a small pink backpack next to your nightstand.

"Who does it belong to?"

"Oh, some girl who is not a good influence. She was bringing me stuff to help me ween off this shit?"

"Well, then why the fuck am I leaving work to bring you kratom, Suboxone, cigarettes, and candy? Why don't you have that junkie bring it to you?"

You hesitated, then said, "I don't even know her name."

"Whatever, Thomas."

Why am I missing work for this shit?

On my way out, I took her pink backpack of stolen make-up and launched it in the air, making sure it landed in the complex dumpster.

And tonight, I showed up at your house and found you asleep. I didn't want to wake you, so I went out to the living room to watch TV. You woke up and found me there eating ice cream with a fork, since all the spoons in your house have disappeared.

"I'm having a panic attack," you said. "I need you to take me to the hospital."

I held your hand the entire drive to Kahului.

We didn't have to wait long to get you into the emergency room, but we waited another hour for the doctor. He was such an asshole talking down to you. He said that if we were in Los Angeles, they would kick your ass out. I glared at him with the attitude of 'you gonna fucking help us or not?' He took X-rays of your lungs, blood samples for STD screening, and a piss test.

I also requested an STD screening. I know it's stupid to put myself in this position, but if you are using needles, I needed to confirm I hadn't contracted anything.

You were given two IV bags to help hydrate and detox.

I was so tired that I curled up next to you on the hospital bed to sleep. The hospital discharged you at one in the morning and didn't provide medication or prescriptions. I feel like the only thing those IV bags helped detox was the Jack in the Box we had for dinner.

October 6, 2016

Dear Thomas,

Yesterday I walked in on something I never want to see. I heard the shower running, so I thought I would join you. I opened the door but you were not in the shower. Instead, I found you standing in front of the mirror with a rubber band around your bicep and pushing a needle in your arm.

"What the fuck are you doing?"

"C'mon, I don't want you to see this shit."

"Stop what you're doing!"

"This is what I do, Danyelle. This is who I am."

I went home crying.

You have no desire to get clean.

"Can I get some cigarettes?" you texted later.

Are you fucking kidding me?

I don't know what it is about you. I have had feelings for you since before your relapse. I know who you are and how wonderful you can be. I know this unfortunate side of you is not the side I fell in love with, but I have hope you will kick this.

"I need to think about it," I replied. "I don't want to, and I'm still upset."

I agreed to buy you cigarettes if you would join me for dinner at our favorite Mexican restaurant. When I pulled into your apartment complex, I messaged, "I'm outside."

"I'll be down in a few minutes. Constipated again."

Whenever you take a while in the bathroom, you share that you're constipated. I hope 'constipated' isn't code for 'I'm in the middle of shooting heroin.'

Dear Thomas,

This morning I reminded you about going to the hospital to detox, and to see if there was a bed available at Maui Rehab. I texted you while at work, "Update please?"

I got a response, but not from you:

"Hi, this is Jenn, Thomas's friend and new roommate! He is trying to get some sleep. He was anxious being in the car. Do you know how long it's been since he has slept?"

This was the bitch you relapsed with three months ago. She was struggling with her own addiction and asking you to sponsor her. My understanding is that men sponsor men and women sponsor women. She obviously has a thing for you to try to convince you to sponsor her and then you end up shooting heroin together. Misery loves company.

"I don't know how long it's been," I replied. "He was probably out all night. So, are you both at the house? Did he not make it to the hospital?"

"He got paranoid in the car. He needs to rest, then I'm taking him there. I know all the nurses. He'll be able to call you but can't have his phone. I'm moving into the other bedroom ASAP. We're just friends and have known each other for over two years. I'm not sure what your relationship is with Thomas but don't worry about him, and me. We decided to move in together to support each other. I went through what he's going through, so I think this is going to be great for both of us. He said you had the only other house key. Can I get that from you at some point today or tonight? And are we sure he's not getting evicted? I was told he was, and he's saying he's not."

Support system, my ass.

Red flags waving.

I let your mom know that this female junkie is untrustworthy. I don't know what Jenn's obsession is with you, but she is wasting her fucking time. I drove to your house as soon as I got off work and had the pleasure of meeting her while you were 'constipated' in the bathroom.

"Is he shooting heroin in there?"

"Oh no, there's no heroin on the island right now?"

Does she think I am that fucking stupid?

"So, how long have you been sober?"

"Two years."

Bullshit.

As she starts blabbing about how she's friends with all the nurses at the hospital and how easy it will be to get you in there, she lights a cigarette and blows the smoke in my face. To say I am disgusted and offended is an understatement. This bitch is straight trash. Who the fuck lights a cancer stick in someone else's house, and in front of someone who doesn't smoke?

You finally came out of the bathroom and smiled like you were happy to see me.

"Hi! Do you want to ride with us to the hospital?"

"You two seem to have everything figured out."

"Oh," you said with a hurt tone.

I shook my head and left. I called your mom and let her know you were going to let this bitch drive you, after everything else I have done for you. The idea was to leave you at the hospital. Was I supposed to drive *with her* back to Lāhainā?

You called hours later for a ride to the hospital.

"What the fuck happened to your friend? I thought she was the perfect chauffeur since she's friends with all the nurses?"

"Fuck her, she just wants to use me for drugs."

"No shit. And I'm supposed to hand over the house key to her?"

We drove to the hospital, got turned away, picked up Jack in the Box, and curled up in bed. It was another night of screaming, shaking, holding you tight, and not sleeping.

October 11, 2016

Dear Thomas,

After another rough night of screaming and shaking, your mom booked a plane ticket to come to Maui. You were supposed to pick her up when she landed. You no-showed and left her stranded at the West Maui airport. She called me as I was getting out of work. It was 3:30 pm and I was already late to babysit. I got to the airport as fast as I could to pick her up.

"How could he *forget* me?"

"He's probably asleep."

We pulled into your apartment complex. I let her know I had to leave immediately because I was late for babysitting, which means my friend was going to be late to her shift.

See how this domino effect works?

You interfere with a lot of people's lives.

I ran your mom's luggage up to the second floor and kicked in your bedroom door to find you asleep, just like I suspected.

"Did you forget about your mom at the airport? *Bye!*"

Since your mom has now been in town the past three days, I have been able to catch up on sleep. She is leaving tomorrow, so she wants me to meet both of you for dinner. Your dad asked her to get a picture with me because he wants to put a face to the angel caring for his son. So sweet. We sent him a photo of me.

"Wow, she is an angel."

October 28, 2016

Dear Thomas,

It hurts me and your family every time you disappear.

We do everything for you: keep a roof over your head, fill the fridge with food, drive you to the hospital, pay for the alcohol to keep you from having seizures, and we lose nights of sleep.

I was driving down Front Street when I saw your truck parked at the crack shack. I called your mom and let her know you were hanging out with the people she calls "the lions."

We are done doing everything for you, Thomas.

You denied being there. You told me you weren't buying drugs, that you were there fixing their air conditioning. Admit it: you fix their AC in exchange for Suboxone, cigarettes, and gas money. I have heard this excuse before. Just buy these assholes a new AC unit because you're over there fixing it all the time. You got defensive and told me the house had ten different rooms and many AC units. Well, allow me to make myself crystal-meth-fucking-clear: when *my* AC unit isn't working, I expect you to come over and fix it.

After everything I have done for you …

You have gone missing again this week, not responding to any calls or messages. I drove by your apartment yesterday, but you weren't there.

"If you don't answer," I texted, "I am going to file a missing person's report."

"I'm in a terrible situation where I owe some crazy people $15, and they are not letting me go. Please don't tell anyone or I'll be in more trouble."

"A little fucking dramatic for $15."

"Yeah, so stupid. It's not your problem."

No shit, it's not my problem.

"Where are you? This isn't funny."

"Can you bring $15 to my house, in the parking lot?"

I drove to your apartment and met you outside.

"So, where are these bad guys holding you hostage?"

"I told them to drive around the block because I didn't want them to see you. And I don't want you to see them. They are dangerous people."

Someone has been watching a little too much TV. The shit that comes out of your mouth is ridiculous. I threw three crumpled Lincoln's at your face and drove away.

November 10, 2016

Dear Thomas,

I spoke with your mom yesterday and she let me know you got into Maui Rehab two days ago. There is a light at the end of the tunnel after all! She sent me the address so I could bring you candy. I know how much you love it when you're detoxing. I drove over an hour to bring you a bag of Li Hing Mui sour apple candies, a few Snickers bars, and a ten-second kiss. Your mom thanked me for giving you love.

"I love your son."

"I know, sweetheart."

Then I spoke with your mom this morning and she let me know you decided to leave Maui Rehab. *After three days?* Why would you do this to yourself, to your family, and to me? You won't give any of us a break. You, of all people, know how difficult it is to get into rehab. There was finally an available bed and you gave it up.

You told your mom you needed me to pick you up at the gas station in Pā'ia. And you sat at that gas station for four more hours, until I got off work.

I barely pulled in and you jumped in the front seat. On the drive home, you said, "I want to get sober on my own."

Wouldn't staying at a treatment center be easier?

We had to pick up your truck, which you had left with Jenn. Why would you lend it to her? How is that junkie worthy of your friendship? Why the *fuck* didn't you have *her* pick you up at the gas station in Pā'ia, with your truck?

She kept dicking us around, saying, "I'm almost there, be there in ten," for *two* hours. Who the fuck does she think she is to be taking her sweet time and wasting ours? I am so fucking livid. Your friends are pathetic and disrespectful.

November 14, 2016

Dear Thomas,

You're staying at my house because you don't like being at your apartment ever since your roommate moved his entire family in and they completely took over. We check on your cat every now and then, and we brought your TV from your place and set it up in my bedroom. I leave work for my "lunch break" almost daily to bring you food, candy, cigarettes, and a couple beers. So much for getting sober on your own.

I haven't been getting much sleep because you like to sleep with the TV on all night, and anytime I am about to finally doze off I hear candy wrappers.

When I am at work, I ask you to do laundry and help around the house for the sake of my roommates. You have helped replace the leaky kitchen sink, replaced two toilet seats, and fixed the creaking screen door, so at least you are keeping busy.

I noticed your favorite pair of board shorts had a giant hole in the back, so I sewed them back together for you. When I told your mom, she thought I was insane.

"You sewed his board shorts? My god, you are an angel."

You didn't notice until I pointed it out.

Your mom constantly texts and calls to let me know how much both she and your dad appreciate what I am doing, and to thank me for loving their son. When she knows you are safe at my house, she is able to sleep better and with a little less worry.

And so, I brought it up again:

"You're still not committing to me being your exclusive

girlfriend? You know I love you, care for you, and think of you as my boyfriend. I have proven myself."

"I know you do. I don't know why, but ever since my ex-girlfriend broke my heart, my heart doesn't feel love. I want to love you, but I don't feel anything."

"I'm sorry, I don't get it. Whitney? What is it about her that ruined you so bad? I'm sorry she broke your heart. I've had my heart broken before, so I know the pain, but you cannot seriously be hung up on someone who broke your heart, what, *eight* years ago?"

You shook your head, and so I brought up another sore topic:

"I know that you crossed paths with her last year and confessed your love to her. She made it clear she was *not* in love with you and that you two would never get back together again. She doesn't give two fucks about you."

You threw an empty beer can across the room.

"That stupid bitch!"

I have never seen you so hurt before and wish you would get past this heartbreak. Some people are going to love you no matter what you do, and some people will never love you no matter what you do. And she does not love you.

November 16, 2016

Dear Thomas,

I found text messages on your phone from Jenn, and it sounds like she came by my house to bring you anxiety medicine when I was asleep. You know how I feel about her and it is extremely disrespectful you would have her come to my house. I'm sick of the "anxiety medicine." It's a crock of shit.

She even texted, "I should've kept your spare keys so we could go for a drive. I'm so sorry you're stuck at Danyelle's house. How about we meet for coffee and figure things out."

Figure *what* out?

What the fuck does she need a spare key for when you have the keys to your truck? If you want to drive around with her, then drive around with her. I don't have you handcuffed to the headboard. You're not stuck at my house. The door is wide open for you to leave when you want. You are obviously forgetting you still have your own apartment, but you enjoy my comfortable house. I blocked her number from contacting you. If you want to stay at my house, then respect me and do *not* contact her anymore.

Later, you were washing your truck in my driveway. I decided to check your phone to make sure you weren't in contact with any of "the lions." I blocked Jenn's phone number but you went around that and had messaged her on Facebook:

"It's been so hard to use my phone. Danyelle pretty much blocked all my contacts."

"I figured she would block my number. What are you gonna do? Do you live with her now? Don't forget you weren't officially evicted legally from your apartment. How's

Salsa? Do you want me to check on the little hairball? Xoxo."

"No, he's good. I'm gonna get everything out by tomorrow so I don't have to continue paying rent."

"You're gonna keep that little furball, right? When can I get cash from you? I have to pay my dealer and I don't have a dollar to cover, otherwise you know I would."

"You can come by tonight cause Danyelle is sleeping now."

"My gas light is on so I can't drive to you. Can you drive to me?"

"Fuck, this is so frustrating. Every time I try to sneak out, Danyelle wakes up. This is the only place I have to stay right now and don't want to jeopardize it. If he could make it to me, that would be awesome."

"My dealer doesn't have a car."

"Fuck, don't know what to do. Danyelle is on super guard right now."

"Erase these messages please."

"Will do. I'm fine with anything he has."

"My friend offered to drive me but now they are acting paranoid. I think they are driving a stolen car."

"Yeah, fuck that."

The messages continued the next day:

"Your phone is doing the same thing. I think I'm still blocked."

"Yeah, that chick Danyelle hijacked my phone and blocked a lot of people."

"Unblock me then. It's annoying."

You are unbelievable, Thomas.

Some *chick?* Is that what I am to you?

You were still washing your truck when I walked outside to put your box of clothes in the front seat and handed you your cellphone.

"Even though I asked you to stop talking to her, you continued. You asked her for more drugs?"

"Why are you going through my phone?"

"You're going to turn this around on *me?* Like what I don't know won't hurt me? Whether I go through your phone or not, you lied to me, disrespected me. You don't need to stay here anymore."

You looked so sad as you coiled up the garden hose.

"Why, Thomas? Why did you do this, after I opened my home to you? Why would you disrespect me like that?"

"Danyelle, I can't give you what you want. I don't know what's wrong with me. My heart just doesn't feel anything for anybody. I see everyone around me in love and I want that so bad but my heart doesn't *feel* love." Then you pounded your chest like you were trying to find a heartbeat to give a fuck, and you started crying. "I can't give you what you want. I'm sorry. You're a wonderful person, you're such a catch, you could have any guy you want—"

I have never seen you cry before.

"Obviously not. Don't give me that 'I can have any guy I want' bullshit. I've made it clear that I have wanted to pursue a relationship with you for a long time now."

You drove away and I ran to my room to cry.

I don't think you realize how hard that was for me. I cried for a while before I called your mom. I apologized to her for kicking you out.

"I *thought* he was fucked up," she said because you had already called her. "I've never heard him cry like that before. He said he wished he could love you the way you love him."

You were crying because you hurt me when that was the last thing you wanted to do. I didn't even know what to say. How could you *not* love me?

I texted you, "I LOVE YOU SO MUCH. Kicking you

to the curb was the hardest thing I have ever had to do. You know I would do anything for you, and I *have*, but you disrespected me. I am so sick to my stomach and terrified for your safety. I want your company. I love your company. And I hate waking up in the middle of the night and you're not there. I pray for you every day and cry every night. I'm not 'some chick' who begs you to block losers' phone numbers. I *am* 'some chick' who feels like their heart went through the fucking garbage disposal."

"Love you too," you texted. "It's too bad my heart was still broken when we met."

Dear Thomas,

I did not sleep well last night. I was worried about your safety. You probably didn't even sleep. You were probably out all night getting drugs. I am so upset about those messages you sent Jenn referring to me as "some chick."

I had a lot to get off my chest, so I sent her a long message:

"Hey! Just so we are crystal-meth-fucking-clear, I have never heard one good thing about you. I didn't like you the second I heard your name. I didn't like you the second I met you. I asked Thomas to stop contacting you because I only have his best interest at heart. I am Team Sober Thomas. Not Team Junkie Thomas. You are a fucking liar and a fucking junkie. If I ever find out you are driving his truck again, I will set it on fire. Thomas is well aware of this. He also knows when you die of your own disease that I will spit on your grave. Thomas was never "stuck" at my house. He is a grown-ass man. If he wanted to leave, he could leave. He wants to be at my house. And now he is devastated that he jeopardized his cushy life in my home and is unwelcome as long as he can't piss clean. You are a big part of that. You messaged him that you were bringing him drugs to my house in a stolen car while I was sleeping. Fuck you. You also asked him to delete those messages. Well, guess what? He didn't. And now those messages are on my phone, so if I ever find out you are anywhere near my house, the cops will be right behind you. When you run out of drugs to give him, I hope your finances cover his truck payment, his gas, his cigarettes. His favorite cereal is Lucky Charms, by the way, and he needs his laundry done every three days. If this is too much, then back the fuck off."

She then tried calling several times, but I ignored her. What the fuck could she possibly have to say? I said what I needed to say. I'm not going to argue with a fruit loop.

I read the message to your parents.

Laughing, they said, "That's our Dani girl."

November 26, 2016

Dear Thomas,

Even though I kicked you out of my house, I still send messages to check on you. Your best friend was nice enough to drop off a futon and a pillow so you can sleep in the back of your truck. Your mom cannot fathom the thought of you sleeping there. If it's that bad, you could go back to your apartment. But if you prefer sleeping in your $30,000 truck over your bedroom in an apartment with roommates, it must not be *that* bad.

Your mom called, begging me to let you sleep at my house, and my answer was no.

"Are you giving up on him?" she said.

"Of course not. I love him and care about him, but this is getting ridiculous. He is *not* homeless. He has a home, he just chooses not to sleep there."

The past two days, you have met me at the gas station across the street from my office for lunch. You even called your mom to let her know.

"Oh, Dani, you are so gentle and kind," she said. "Thank you for not giving up on him. You are an angel!"

Then you asked me to pay off a drug debt and get your dive watch back, which you had used for collateral. You told me it was a drug debt from a couple months ago, but I saw you wearing that watch a few days ago. This isn't an old debt, it's a *new* drug debt.

My *hānai* sister Piper is out of town this Thanksgiving. I thought it would be nice for you to sleep over with me at her house since it would be empty for a few days. We picked up groceries and cooked dinner and fell asleep while watching a movie, like old times.

I left for work this morning and left you sleeping at Piper's. I didn't realize her boyfriend was planning to move her furniture to his house. Had I known, I would have made sure you left the same time I did.

"How long has Thomas been staying in my house?"

Piper was furious. I instantly became sick to my stomach. I don't ever put myself in situations like this. I didn't even know what to say.

I tried to convince her it was okay and you were going to help move her furniture. After another text from her, I couldn't face it and didn't respond. I had betrayed her trust and feel awful. I just want to turn my phone off and run away.

November 29, 2016

Dear Thomas,

I found out your property manager served you an eviction notice over a month ago. You have to move everything out tomorrow. Your mom is stressing out about it and I am frustrated because I offered to help sell your furniture months ago:

"You're always needing money for cigarettes and gas, so sell it!"

Your mom has been adamant about keeping everything so we can furnish your next home. She's holding onto this idea of you still having a normal living situation.

This tangible shit is *not* important.

Your mom ended up getting you a storage unit, which you will fill with your furniture tomorrow. And don't forget you have a cat.

December 19, 2016

Dear Thomas,

You were evicted from your apartment, so your mom spent money on a hotel room. It never stops. She loves you so much but as long as she continues to make your life as manageable as possible, you will never hit rock bottom. I am guilty for it too. I have been called everything in the book: an enabler, codependent. Where and how do you draw the line between enabling someone and loving them? It's a blurry line and I don't know how to clear it up. I wish you were sober so you could be the one to explain it to me.

Your parents don't have a lot of money, so the hotel stay ended after a week and you setup a campsite a few miles south of Lāhainā. I brought my laptop and a DVD with me, so we had a cozy movie night camping on the beach. We made the best of it.

I have been buying gallon water jugs for you, but you call me every day telling me you're out because you've been using the water to bathe. And you ask me to bring new water jugs every time I drive out to your campsite.

"Stop throwing the empty jugs in the trash," I told you, "and refill them. You have quarters in the truck. Refill the jugs at the store. You don't have anywhere else to be."

After that last encounter, I didn't hear from you for a few days. I went by your campsite and found you asleep in your tent. I noticed a trail of foam on the air mattress, on your chest, and coming out of your mouth. I lifted your head and screamed, "Oh my god, did you have a seizure?" And then I discovered the cup of melted Oreo McFlurry.

I sighed with relief, then looked down and saw the pile of needles.

I don't even feel anger anymore, only frustration.

You were mad because I shared that discovery with your mom. You said it was my fault she was losing sleep and that I shouldn't have told her. You made me feel guilty, even though I know we would *all* be sleeping better if you wouldn't stick needles in your arm.

Another three days went by and you still hadn't come by to pick up the laundry I had washed for you on my day off. You called while I was at my storage unit. I said to meet me there and to call because your clothes were in the back of my car. An hour went by.

"Where are you? Are you coming by or not?"

"I already did. I grabbed my clothes from your car."

What?

My car was locked.

I looked and sure enough your clothes were gone.

"I gotta go," you said, "bye."

You didn't bother to thank me. Fuck you. I have gone above and beyond for you, and I will not take this disrespect any longer. I called your mom and let her know I was done with you. I have been bending over backward for you the past five months, and for what?

And then I received a text message from you this morning that read, "I just wanted to tell you thank you so much for being such a good friend. You've done so much for me and I will never forget that. If you ever need anything, please give me a call."

I will no longer be answering your phone calls or text messages. Trust me, Thomas, if I ever need anything, you will be the last person I call.

February 24, 2017

Dear Thomas,

It took a lot to finally cut all communication with you. Between July through December, while I was babysitting you, I gained forty pounds. I completely neglected my health. I have spent endless nights staying up with you, holding you to keep you from shaking, sleeping with one eye open to make sure you weren't meeting drug dealers, and late-night runs to the liquor store for cigarettes and alcohol. I was eating nothing but fast food with you.

My hair started falling out as well from stress and lack of sleep. How is it you're the one shooting drugs into your veins but it's causing my hair loss?

I have been skinny my entire life. When I look in the mirror now, I am disgusted with myself. I don't even recognize who I am anymore. My self-esteem is so low. I look like a whale and I'm missing chunks of hair. The entire time I have been catering to you and sleeping at your house, we weren't having sex. Besides the few nights you'd fall asleep with your arms around me, you wouldn't touch me. This was not helping my self-esteem. I'm fat, balding, unattractive, and you not wanting to have sex with me validates how physically unattractive I have become.

The past two months of zero communication with you have been peaceful, until this afternoon when your mom texted, "Dani, Thomas wants you to call him. I just got off the phone with him. Would you please call him? Love you."

What the fuck for? She texted me several more times begging me to call you. I waited an hour until I clocked out of work.

"Hi!"

"Hi?"

"I thought I was never going to speak to you again."

"Yeah, that's the idea."

We spoke for a few minutes. You told me you were sorry after I told you exactly what hurt me the most and what was fueling my nightmares: the horrible things you said about me and how you painted pictures of me to insignificant people, the fact that you told people I am clingy and psycho for going into your phone and blocking drug dealers' phone numbers.

Everything I did was always for your best interest and wellbeing. How you treated me was unbelievably disrespectful and it fucking hurt. I don't know how to be your friend, Thomas.

I want all of you, but I am lonely and heartbroken.

Dear Thomas,

Barbara called on Monday. She is done supporting you living on Maui. If you are going to continue to call your parents for money, you can move to Kona. She asked if I could take you to the airport and I gladly accepted. You are adamant about not moving there.

You met me at the gas station for lunch and asked me to help with your taxes so you could live off the refund, but what happens when that money runs out? You handed me your W2 and I filed your taxes that evening. Your refund came to $2,516. Your mom and I decided to send your refund via paper check to Kona.

Yes, we blackmailed you into moving there.

She was nervous that she was going to pay for a plane ticket and you weren't going to show. She also purchased a plane ticket for me to personally deliver you.

When your mom greeted us, I hugged her and thanked her for paying for our flight. You were more in a hurry to light your cigarette than give her a hug.

It was weird for me staying with you in Kona.

We hardly spoke on the flight, we have hardly spoken in the last three months, and now we were spending the night in your room. Somehow, we fell asleep cuddling.

Your mom loves seeing us together. She loves seeing someone (me) love her son. She's seen you get your heart broken and she's always pushed for you to move on from that heartache. She's always wanted and wondered when you were going to find your person.

I love you, which is no secret to you or your family.

Overall, it was a good couple of days. You gave me the

tour around Kona and showed me where you hung out and made trouble as a kid. I enjoyed bonding with Barbara in the kitchen while she taught me how to make French toast. Afterward, it was nice flipping through photo albums and sipping coffee with your parents.

When it was time for me to fly back to Maui, you told me you didn't want me to leave.

Dear Thomas,

Your mom called. She is sick of you.

"His tax refunds arrived, but when he deposited them into his account, the bank kept the money because he's so far behind on his truck payments. Thomas is disrespectful and not getting sober. If he wants to go back to Maui so bad, he should go. I'm done with him."

I picked you up from the airport Wednesday morning. You lifted me up and spun me around with an unexpected and exciting greeting: "Dani, I love you!"

Did you just tell me you love me?

While driving home, you were dramatically happy, which is usually when you're trying to hide something.

"You're high."

"No, I'm not."

"Yes, you are. You're definitely not sober."

"Baby, I haven't used any drugs since before I left for the big island."

I'm supposed to be excited that you're back on Maui, that you're going to be staying with me, and you finally realize you love me, but you seemed high.

I called your mom when we got home, crying.

"He's fucked up."

"That's not possible. I drove him to the airport and you were there waiting for him. When would he have time to get drugs?"

"I'm not sure, but if I've learned anything, it's that he is capable of getting creative when he wants to score."

You then asked me to drive you to the crack shack because "the lions" owed you money. Are you insane? Do you think I'm stupid? How do drug dealers owe you money?

"I was selling drugs for them before I left Maui."

"You *use* drugs, you don't *sell* drugs. I'm not taking you there. Fuck you."

I drove us to my house and as soon as we pulled into the driveway, you walked down the street to the crack shack. I shook my head.

What am I doing?

I'm assuming you're going to sleep there now. You did what you had to do to get a flight to Maui and a ride to Lāhainā. Why did your mom allow you to fly back? She was so adamant last month getting you to Kona. Now she has dumped this problem on me.

About an hour went by and you came back home, seemingly not any more fucked up. You said you walked in there, threw a few punches to let everyone know you were back, and came back to give me a $100 bill. You've been back for less than two hours and you've already exhausted me.

You have been sweating and detoxing each night, not getting much sleep. You had bad anxiety last night, so I suggested we walk around the neighborhood. There was one particular house you weren't comfortable passing because you owed someone money there.

Like I give a shit.

If you're too paranoid to walk around our own neighborhood, then why did you come back to Maui? I'm not giving in to this dramatic paranoia.

This morning when I left for work, I decided to leave you my cellphone. This way your mom could get ahold of you and I could get ahold of you while at work. You went to a morning meeting and then drove to Kīhei about an hour away. I looked up your location with Find My iPhone. You stayed in one spot all day in Kīhei and were still there when

I left work, but when I got home you were watching TV in my room. Without hesitation, you confessed that you had left my phone at a gas station.

"What the fuck? When did you realize that?"

"I was already halfway back to Lāhainā."

"And you didn't turn around to get it?"

May 9, 2017

Dear Thomas,

Barbara asked us to empty the storage unit and move everything to my backyard. She wants you to hold onto the shit so you'll have a furnished apartment once you get sober, get a job, and put your life back together. She is no longer going to pay for storage. I thought it was stupid in the first place and suggested selling your furniture months before you were evicted. But when you rolled up the door, you revealed an empty unit.

"Where is your furniture?"

"I took it to the pawn shop to buy drugs."

"When?"

"A while ago."

"So, your mom has been paying $180 a month to store nothing?"

"I didn't want to tell her I got rid of the furniture. She wanted me to keep it."

"So, you thought it was better to waste her money?"

Unbelievable.

Later I was making the bed and found a thick rubber band under your pillow, the kind you use to tie around your bicep to find a vein. When I confronted you about it, you said you weren't using drugs, and that you'd found it in your stuff.

"I didn't want anyone to see it in the trash, so I stashed it under the pillow."

First, you're an idiot because you know I make my bed every day. Second, I don't give a shit what anyone sees in the trash. What matters is that it's trash!

Days later, I found the cap of a needle in the laundry.

"It must have been in my pocket," you said, "from a long time before."

I can't ignore the other signs.

You've been sweating and detoxing. You're not sleeping. You toss and turn, and you flinch. You constantly make a frown face or stick your tongue out without control. When half asleep, you smack or pucker your lips, and grunt. You constantly lift your legs in the air and arch your back, and it looks like your hands are always in a cramped position.

Sleeping next to you is distracting and restless. I woke up one night and you were nowhere to be found. It was raining and your truck was in the driveway, but you were gone. This made me frantic because you have a history of seizures. I searched for you in the backyard with my flashlight in the pouring rain. I imagined you went out for a smoke, had a seizure, and fell in the dirt. Then I realized my car was gone.

You returned twenty minutes later. I was in full panic.

"Where did you go? You had me worried sick!"

"I went to the gas station. You were asleep. I didn't want to wake you."

"Leave a fucking *note*."

"I'm sorry, I didn't think you'd wake up."

Last night escalated when I woke up to screaming. Weird, different screaming. You were not in bed next to me. I searched through the house, but you weren't in the bathroom, and you weren't in the living room. I found you on the kitchen floor crammed up against a wall. Looking like someone pretending to make baby noises, you were flipping your wrist and cooing. It was so fucking strange. I yanked on your arm to get up.

"What the fuck are you doing?!"

You sat up straight and seemed to "sober up" in a second.

"What was I doing?"

"Why are you so fucked up?"

"Maybe I was sleepwalking."

"You cannot sleep in my house if you're screaming and waking up my roommates."

I gave you a pillow to sleep in your truck.

May 11, 2017

Dear Thomas,

Last night was nothing short of dramatic, chaotic, and stressful. You kept me up the entire night after I asked you a hundred times to go to bed. You were disrupting everyone, constantly walking in and out of the house, acting sketchy as fuck. I followed you and told you to get in bed or not come back inside at all.

I went outside and you had a yellow spider box, one of those portable power distribution devices. You used my phone to google how much it was worth. You said you had to take it to your friends down the street, right away … *at two in the morning*. You got on my roommate's bike and rode down the street, struggling for balance. I shook my head, wondering what the hell was I witnessing. I went back inside to sleep but that never happened. I had to wake up at 5:30 to walk to Lāhainā Harbor. You still had not gone to bed. I was scheduled to get on a ferry at 6:15 to go to Lānaʻi with a coworker.

I forced myself into a state of denial so I could enjoy the day, and my coworker accepted my denial for me. We both decided that if my house caught fire, there was nothing I could do about it anyway. I was on a boat between the islands of Maui and Lānaʻi and wouldn't be back for at least eight hours. I turned off my phone.

Whatever problems were going on in my life, they didn't need to exist today.

When I got back to Lāhainā, I turned my phone back on. I had angry text messages from my neighbor because you stole his backpack with his prescription sunglasses. My roommates said there were six cop cars at the construction site across the street, and fliers with photos of a stolen yellow spider box worth $800.

I didn't know where you were or who you're with but I had a suspicion to search my room to make sure there wasn't anything there that shouldn't be. Under the pillows: nothing. In the nightstand: nothing. Back of the closet: nothing. And then I checked your jacket hanging outside the closet and unzipped the pocket: *four needles*. I tore my bathroom apart, and under the sink: *bottle caps stuffed with wet cotton*.

Now I'm sitting in my house fuming, waiting for you to come around so I can kick you right back out. There is absolutely nothing you can say or do to change my mind.

After a couple more hours, you finally walked into the house and I told you to get out. I followed you and we went for a drive.

"I threw away all the needles I found in my room and all your other junkie shit. I know you stole from our neighbor this morning; the cops were outside today looking for the spider box you stole. Last night was unacceptable and you are *not* welcome here anymore."

You started crying, kicking, and screaming, like a child.

"Where am I supposed to go?"

"I don't care."

"You want me to be homeless?"

The guilt-tripping did not make this easier. I am *not* at fault here. You are the creator of your own misery. You have lied and stolen from everyone who cares about you. I am no longer feeling strong or confident and that is because I have a heart. I have compassion and empathy for you, but there is a line to be drawn.

You cried and screamed even louder, making it more painful.

I got out of your truck and walked home.

When I got there, another one of my roommates caught me in his arms.

"This isn't fun!" I said, crying. "I did not want to do that!" Then I locked myself in my room and sobbed, heartbroken, *again*.

May 22, 2017

Dear Thomas,

After I kicked you out a second time, you snuck around the side of the house and tapped on my bedroom window. I have never had anyone do that before. I always thought it would be nice to have a cute guy tap on my window like in the movies, holding a boombox over his head, but not under these circumstances. You wanted food and water, like a feral cat.

Your mom sends text messages all the time letting me know you're starving and thirsty. She guilt-trips me into meeting you for breakfast or lunch.

"If he's so hungry," I told her, "why doesn't he rob a grocery store?"

A grocery store doesn't have feelings to hurt.

I came home from a party to find you in my driveway. You wanted your dive gear to pay for a drug debt. I lied and told you it was locked away in a storage unit we didn't have access to late at night. Your dive gear was in the trunk of my car, three feet away.

"I need a hundred dollars."

"No. I don't have a hundred dollars."

When you look at me, you don't see a loving girlfriend, you see "automated teller machine."

"It's just a hundred dollars."

"*Just* a hundred dollars? A hundred dollars every other day for ten months is $15,000 in cigarettes, Nicotine gum, alcohol, food, and gas. Let's not forget your parents were paying your rent and truck payment. What about the $1,000 your mom wasted on that empty storage unit?"

"You and my mom are not compassionate."

"Are you fucking kidding me?"

A couple days later, you stole my roommate's skateboard to pawn off and you stole my Ryobi drill set, which I found but had to buy back. I never would have imagined you stealing from me. After everything I have done for you …

You recently destroyed one of your tires, so your truck is parked down the street with only three. Your mom called me and asked if I would help pick up a fourth tire for you.

"I'll buy it," she said.

"For what? He doesn't have a job. He doesn't need to be anywhere. Where the fuck does he need to drive?"

"Well, it can't just sit on the side of the road."

"He doesn't need a $30,000 truck. He is months behind on his payments. How has it not already been repossessed?"

I have no idea who brought the tire your mom purchased for your fancy Toyota Tacoma, but someone did, because I saw you driving around town. But that didn't last long.

I got a phone call from your mom not much later.

"Someone stole his truck!"

I couldn't help but laugh.

Well, if it still only had three tires …

The cops eventually found your truck, but the bank made sure to repo it and now it's gone forever, along with the new tire.

May 30, 2017

Dear Thomas,

I have been ignoring calls from random phone numbers all week. I was clocking in at work when another random 808 number called. I would have liked to ignore it but it was time to tell you to stop.

"Hello?" I answered grumpily.

"Oh sorry, I must have the wrong—"

"No, you don't, Thomas."

"Can I get some food and cigarettes?"

"I can't do this anymore. I'm done. No more cigarettes, no more alcohol, no more money. This isn't fair. Don't call me anymore."

"Oh sorry, I won't bother you."

"You don't get to talk to me like that. Seriously, this is so hard for me, but I cannot enable you anymore. Please, *please*, just get help."

"I'm sorry."

"Don't call me anymore. Get help."

I hung up, upset knowing I had to. Then I looked at the date on my phone: May 30th. My face fell into the palm of my hands and I cried hysterically. It's your birthday.

Sick to my stomach, I immediately called back, praying you'd answer.

"Hello?"

"I'm sorry I am so upset, but I wanted to tell you happy birthday."

Silence, then a shaken, "Thank you."

"I wish today was different, but I cannot do this anymore."

"I know, I'm sorry."

"I love you, Thomas."

"I love you too."

The silent pause and your shaky voice let me know you didn't remember it was your birthday.

August 3, 2017

Dear Thomas,

I have not spoken to you since I broke up with you on your birthday. I still cry every night not knowing where you are, wondering if you have a safe place to sleep. I don't doubt your parents are still sending you money. I haven't talked to your mom because it's too painful, and I hadn't heard from your dad until today.

"Aloha."

"Hi, Dani."

"Hi, Tom, how are you?"

"Well, we flew into Maui today to pick up Thomas. We pulled him out of the bushes and took him to the hospital. He has a bad staph infection."

"Oh."

"Dani, we need his birth certificate and medical card so we can fly him back to Kona with us. Any way we can get that from you?"

I forgot your personal documents were at my house.

"Okay, I am babysitting right now. I have to work in the morning, so I guess I'll have to bring them to you tonight."

"That would be great. We are at the hospital now. We are staying at a hotel on Ka'ahumanu Avenue."

As I drove to Kahului, my mind spun. *Am I going to see you? Do I go into the hospital room? Do I stay in the lobby? Do I even leave my car?* Seeing you will be too hard for me, I realized, so I called your dad when I arrived.

"I am outside the lobby, Tom. Don't let Thomas know I am here."

I handed over everything to your dad, a hundred feet away, and your mom and your friend were assisting you into the car. After all this time, after all the pain, all the bullshit, you're dirty and haggard as fuck, yet I still get butterflies when I see you.

I walked over and gave your mom a hug, said hello to her and only her, and saw you throwing back a bottle of vodka. Right outside the emergency room. Typical. You didn't even notice I was there.

"Thomas, Dani is here," Barbara said. "Say hi."

I let her know, "No, I'm good."

Your friend whispered into your ear and pointed at me.

"Dani! Dani! Come here! I just want my girl!"

Hearing you scream for me is something I had never experienced. My eyes filled with water, my heart heavy.

"Dani, Dani! Come hug me, please! I love you!"

I leaned into the car for a hug and you would not let go.

"I am so happy you're here! I missed you so much! I love you!"

I wiggled free and looked at your mom.

"I'm gonna have to stay at the hotel with you, huh?"

"Yes, you are," Barbara said and smiled. "Thomas, Dani is going to meet us at the hotel."

"No, she's coming with us!"

"I have my own car I need to drive." Then you grabbed onto me again, so I said, "Babe, I promise I will be there. It's five minutes away. I'll see you in five minutes."

At the hotel not much later, I scanned the parking lot for your parents' rental car. Everyone standing around the car had a stressed look on their face. You were throwing a fit and apparently wouldn't get out until I arrived. When your superwoman arrived, everyone was ready to walk to the hotel room but you were holding onto the moment.

"Come on, Thomas," everyone was saying.

"Just let me hold my girl."

"Yes, she is your girl, and she is here, now let's all head up to the room."

"Just let me hold my girl, just let me hold my girl."

"Yeah, yeah, but let's all head—"

"Everyone shut up, *please*," you said, "Just let me hold her. She is my queen and I have missed her so much!"

I don't think I have ever felt this much love from you until now. For two years, you kept your guard up and fed me excuses that you don't feel love and your heart is incapable of loving someone. I was determined to show you how much I love and care for you.

We made our way to the room. The hospital gave you an antibiotic shot in the ass for your staph infection before discharging you, but they did not bother cleaning the infection on your foot and leg. They didn't even put a bandage on it. They did absolutely nothing. Another sad example of a hospital discriminating against a homeless drug addict.

After living on the streets, in the bushes, and on the beach the last two months, you were filthy. I put you in the bathtub and you curled up, leaning onto the wall side of the tub, moaning in agony as I scrubbed the dirt from your back, arms, and torso. I took my time scrubbing the infected leg and foot. I was finishing bathing you when you looked at me and leaned in for the sweetest kiss on the lips.

"I thought I was never going to see you again," you said.

Dear Thomas,

I flew to Kona last night just to see you, knowing things were tense between you and your mom. While getting dressed that first morning, you walked in and with a tone as casual as if asking me to order a pizza said, "Hey, can you call 911 when you have a moment?"

When I have a moment?

You don't wait for a moment to call 911.

You make calling 911 the moment.

"What? Why?"

You found your mom in bed, nearly glowing yellow. Her tiny body had swollen so large she physically appeared six months pregnant.

The paramedics arrived and drove her away in the ambulance. I was in her bedroom gathering anything she might need at the hospital when I found her wallet on the floor next to her nightstand. I got on my knees to retrieve it and discovered a dozen empty beer bottles under her side of the bed. To salvage her dignity, I threw them away.

We drove to the emergency room to be with her. The doctor wasn't available to start taking tests for several hours. When her lab results came through for her liver, we were told the average ALT units per liter should be between seven and thirty-five. Barbara's was over 800.

Your mom's alcoholism has caught up with her.

She has Cirrhosis, a chronic disease of the liver, and the hospital is not admitting her to a room because she needs a medivac to O'ahu immediately.

September 21, 2017

Dear Thomas,

I was with you for five days last month. I made sure to leave you plenty of food and water because your dad was on Oʻahu with your mom. They were gone for two weeks before returning to Kona. I'm back there now for another five-day "vacation." When you picked me up from the airport, I asked on the drive home, "How have things been the past couple weeks?"

"Weird."

"What is weird about being home with your parents?"

"My entire life, for as long as I can remember, my mom has always been buzzed or drunk. I've never seen her sober before. I look at her, and she's my mom, but I feel like I'm living with a stranger."

Saturday marked her one month of sobriety and she asked me to give her a pedicure to celebrate. I setup a soaking tub on the lanai and did my best shaping her nails. She wanted her toenails to be painted fiery red.

"Aren't you proud of your mom for being sober thirty days?"

"She's only sober because the doctors told her she'd die if she drinks again. Thirty days is nothing. Try being sober for almost five years."

"You are so mean to each other. This is a huge milestone for her! When was the last time *you* were sober for thirty days? When was the last time you were sober for *one?*"

We drove to Papakōlea Beach the next day. It was too windy for swimming, but I loved sitting there with my toes in the green sand. On our way home, we stopped at the grocery store to pick up ingredients your mom requested for dinner. You were too tired, so I went inside the store alone. When I returned to the truck, I noticed the cap of a needle inside the door compartment. It was not there before I left to shop.

"You're really doing this to me right now?"

"Doing what?"

I pulled the cap out from the door.

"That's not mine."

"Then where the fuck did it come from?"

"I don't know."

Unbelievable. I didn't bother arguing and ignored you the rest of the ride home.

Whenever I give you the silent treatment, you try extra hard to give me attention. You try to be cute and rub my neck while I drive. You snuggle with me more while we're watching TV. I know what you're trying to do. You're trying to apologize for hurting your loved ones by showing affection. It doesn't make me forget everything that has happened.

Barbara cooked the first few nights I was there. One night she wanted to dress up and take us out for a fancy steak dinner. A family night out to make memories together sounded nice. When it was time to go, you refused to get up from your hangover-induced nap. You weren't budging, so we left you behind. It's sad you have zero interest in spending time with the people who love you most.

You were still sleeping when we got home. I slept in the spare bedroom and heard you get up to smoke. You didn't check on me, didn't care that I wasn't sleeping next to you.

For my entire visit, you paid every time we went out to eat. A nice treat, but where did you get the money?

Barbara asked me yesterday, "Have you been paying for everything?"

"No, he has."

"Cash or card?"

"Cash."

"Where has he been getting the money?"

"I thought you gave him the cash."

With further research, Barbara realized every time she gave you her bank card for groceries, you took it to another level, taking advantage of "cash back" at the register. You've been piling up cash to spend on me but to also visit your drug dealers.

It was my last full day to be with you, but you disappeared for several hours. I sat on the front steps waiting for you and called multiple times.

"You understand today is the last day we get to spend together?" I asked when you finally answered. "I don't know when I get to see you again."

It was my last night in Kona, so when you returned home I expected that you'd want to be intimate, but you wouldn't even cuddle. Whenever I try to have sex, you tell me you don't feel good or make excuses, which kills my self-esteem and makes me feel unattractive.

Then you woke your dad up at two in the morning and made him drive you to the emergency room. It's your second favorite place to be besides the liquor store. You get drunk, can't handle the withdrawals, so you go to the hospital for an IV to help with the tremors. And the first thing you do when you leave is buy more alcohol to repeat the cycle.

You were at the hospital for maybe thirty minutes before you called your dad to come back. The nurses kicked you out. They know your games. I was selfishly excited you were rejected because I could spend a few more hours with you. I skipped breakfast, kissed you goodbye, and then Tom dropped me off at the airport.

Dear Thomas,

We have hardly spoken the past six weeks. You've been in and out of the Kona hospital. You're usually detoxing but recently you've been fighting an infection. I have called your hospital room several times but the nurses tell me you're not in the mood to talk. You didn't call me on my birthday. I didn't hear from your parents either.

Your mom called two days ago to inform me you were arriving in Maui.

"What? Why?" I'm not ready for the shitshow.

"Dani, this is a medivac. His kidneys are failing. He is being flown to Maui Memorial because the Kona ICU does not have a dialysis machine."

"I will visit him tonight."

"Honey, Thomas will be asleep."

"I'll wake him up when I get there."

"No, honey. He's in a coma."

"What?"

"He has been in an induced coma for more than two weeks."

"Why did no one tell me?"

I was babysitting all day yesterday so I couldn't see you during daytime visitor hours. I called to confirm I was allowed to visit after eight. I arrived at the hospital at 7:15. I waited, and waited, and waited. At 7:55, the security guard finally told me I needed a visitor's pass.

I have never visited anyone in an intensive care unit before. I have never *had* anyone to visit in ICU.

A nurse set me up with a hospital gown and gloves because, I was informed, you have *Clostridioides difficile*, also known as *C. diff*, which she told me is highly contagious. I didn't know what to expect, but your nurse tried to prepare me for what I was about to see.

There you were, unconscious, with every possible machine connected to you: breathing tube, feeding tube, catheter. Your entire body swollen. Your hands triple their regular size. Your wrists strapped down to the bed.

"It's so he doesn't pull out his breathing tube while he's asleep," the nurse explained.

"How serious is this infection?"

"It's a nasty one."

"We're not going to lose him, are we?"

"No. He will be okay."

I looked at you and sighed, taking it all in.

"Oh baby, what have you done to yourself now? Please tell me you're done with this shit. What else needs to happen for you to get sober?"

I kissed the top of your head and whispered, "Please wake up."

Dear Thomas,

One of my best friends, Bryan, flew in last night. I went to visit you before picking him up from the airport. I got to the hospital early to get my visitors pass and patiently waited outside the ICU doors. At eight o'clock, I buzzed the nurses to let me in, but no one answered. I waited five minutes before buzzing again. No answer. I peeked through the window of the ICU doors and I could see the doctors and nurses rushing to a room. Clearly someone was dying and letting me through the door was understandably not a priority. Another thirty minutes passed before I started crying because I don't take any moment with you for granted.

The hospital Chaplain rolled by in a wheelchair.

"Are you okay?" he asked.

"No. I am here to visit my boyfriend, but no one is letting me in. I understand there's an emergency, but I just need the door to unlock. I can dress myself in the gown and gloves."

His wife recognized me from getting my visitor's pass forty-five minutes prior. The Chaplain has access to the ICU rooms, so he confirmed it was okay for me to enter.

"What's your boyfriend's name?"

"Thomas."

"Does Thomas know you're here?"

"It's hard to say. He's been in a coma for three weeks."

"Talk to him. He can hear you."

November 14, 2017

Dear Thomas,

Your friend Lacey, who works at the hospital, texted me yesterday: "Thomas is awake. He is confused and lethargic. Not talking, but mouthing words."

I am sad I wasn't there for you at that moment, but after twenty-three days in an induced coma, I am so happy to know you are finally awake.

I couldn't wait to visit you today. I ran through the hallway to throw on my gown and gloves. Your eyes lit up when I grabbed your hand and kissed you on your forehead like I did the first time I saw you in the ICU.

You could barely put words together but you managed to mutter "shitty apple juice" because the nurse waters it down to limit your sugar intake. You kept scratching your beard because you always have a clean-shaven face. You would never in a million years grow a beard. I had asked the nurses if I could shave your face when you were still in the coma, but they said it was too risky. I drove the nurses nuts while you were in the coma:

"Excuse me, can we clean his face? He's drooling."

"He needs a new pillowcase."

"He needs a fresh gown."

"The machine is beeping again."

"When is his next sponge bath?"

I made sure you were well taken care of.

You were irritated today because the nurses started to cut back on your pain medication. There is one particular nurse who is nice and great at her job but she is unapologetically loud. There are patients in every ICU room trying to rest but she makes it impossible.

"If you're not going to give him a Valium," I snapped at her, "could you lower your fucking voice?"

She looked at me in shock and left us alone. You smiled and asked me to play meditation recordings and massage your scalp.

Later the nurse brought your dinner.

I asked, "Can you feed yourself or do you need me to feed you?"

"You can feed me."

I laughed and said, "Okay, your majesty."

Dear Thomas,

I was at work counting down the hours until I could visit you at the hospital. Then your dad called to let me know he got a phone call from your nurse.

You escaped ICU?

You were in a coma for twenty-three days. You woke up four days ago, were only able to stand three days ago, learned to walk two days ago, and now you're running out the fire exit?

Somebody is lying. This does not make sense.

You have no clothes, no shoes, no phone, no ID. I couldn't help but imagine the catheter on your arm and the tube going from that catheter to your heart. I'm waiting for a photo of you walking around Wailuku in a hospital gown with your butt cheeks out to be posted to social media.

Tom bought a plane ticket to fly you back to Kona, but you didn't have your ID to get on the plane. I told your dad, "It's on the floor, under his side of the bed."

He drove your ID to the Kona airport and paid the Mokulele pilot to take it with him on the next flight to Maui so you could get on the exact plane and fly back to Kona with your ID in your pocket *because that is how I get shit done!*

Dear Thomas,

Your mom called to tell me she is dying.

I immediately booked a flight to Kona to have my chance to say goodbye. I flew in last night and picked up my rental car. Your dad gave me the heads-up that you would not be at the house because you were back in the hospital, *again*. I can't believe I haven't spoken to you since before you ran out of the ICU on Maui. And I can't believe I heard that you attempted to pull the tube out of your arm ... what that must have been like, what it must have *looked* like.

I slept in without an alarm, took my time getting ready this morning, stopped at a coffee shop, and then made my way to the Kona hospital. I walked into the lobby and grabbed the wall phone connected to the operator.

"I need the room number for Walker."

"Which Walker?"

"Both."

I was there to visit your mom. She's dying so I was planning to spend time with her and say my goodbyes. You didn't deserve a visit from me.

I started second-guessing myself inside the elevator. *Do I visit you before Barbara in case you're discharged? Shit.* I decided to stop by your room first.

Your eyes grew wide because you didn't know I was in Kona.

"Hello." I was snarky. After all those late-night visits I spent with you in the ICU, you had the audacity to run out of there without saying goodbye.

"Hi," you said and leaned in to kiss me. "I got into a treatment center on O'ahu. I'm going this week."

"That's good."

"When did you get here?"

"Last night."

"How did you get here?"

"An airplane."

"I mean … to the hospital. Did my dad drop you off?"

"I rented a car."

"Could you give me a ride to the store to get some beer?"

"You *just said* you're going to rehab!"

"I am, I just need a beer to help me relax before I go."

"I am here to visit Barbara. I just wanted to let you know I'm here."

You followed me, like a puppy, out of your room. I was waiting for the elevator when the nurses stopped you.

"Are you leaving?" one of them asked you.

"No."

The nurses looked at each other with annoyed faces.

"I am going to visit my mom downstairs."

"Do not leave without being discharged!" one of them said, adamant.

The nurses are familiar with your bullshit. They are sick and tired of treating you, especially when you have left without being discharged many times before.

Your mom was pleased to see us together.

Barbara looked different but absolutely beautiful. No longer swollen. She was sober, her hair exceptionally blonde.

I'm savoring this time with her if the end is near.

I was talking with Barbara when you kept poking me and whispering, "Can we leave to get some beer?" I tried to ignore you. We spent fifteen minutes with her and you were bugging me the entire time to leave. You are worse than a screaming toddler. You are so selfish. You don't think about anyone's needs except your own.

I decided I would come back later to visit with her more. As we walked out the door, I turned my head and shouted to her, "You look good!"

After we left your mom at the hospital, we picked up your stupid beer. You swore you only needed two and that would be enough. I asked what date and time you needed to check into treatment on Oʻahu and you said you could show up anytime during the weekend.

Someone finally called and asked if you could arrive in the next few hours, but that was a hard no. You lost your State ID, *again!* How were you supposed to board a plane?

I drove us to the DMV, knowing we needed your social security card and two proofs of address. You have been homeless for almost a year. No bills. No cellphone. No auto insurance. No internet. No cable. No water. No electricity. No responsibilities. However, you *do* have a massive pile of medical bills.

The woman behind the DMV counter said we needed another proof of address. Multiple hospital bills from multiple hospitals did not suffice.

Are you fucking kidding me?

"Ma'am, this situation is extremely imperative. He is going to rehab, and he needs to be able to get on the plane, today. That is why we are here."

She wouldn't help us. It was frustrating, but I wasn't going to let her get in my way. I was on a mission. I'd use your dad's mail as proof of address since you have the same first and last name. When we got back to the house, I went through his desk, only to find his mail is addressed to him with his middle initial. You don't have the same middle initial. I felt defeated and unaccomplished. And you spent the rest of the day *begging* me to buy more alcohol.

"Baby, can we go to the store? I need another beer."

"No."

"Baby, please. Just one more."

"No!"

"Baby, please, *please*, just one more beer. I swear just one more. It will help me stop shaking, baby, *please*, I need another beer, just *one* more, *please* …"

This went on for half an hour.

I tried to ignore you, but you only made me cry.

This was draining on so many levels, and you were literally sitting on your hands and knees begging me to go to the store, looking right into my eyes with tears falling.

"Shut up! Leave me alone!"

"Baby, *please*, I will leave you alone after you go to the store."

You broke me.

Every person who has ever called me an enabler should know they wouldn't have lasted five minutes listening to you beg. They would have caved in less than three to give you what you wanted. Or they would have abandoned you. Something I am clearly incapable of doing.

All your friends have abandoned you. I am the only one fighting to keep you alive.

So, I got you your fucking beer.

A lot of beer.

You got so drunk you couldn't stand. I watched you, a 5'11", 220-pound drunk, fall and hit the back of your head on the papasan chair. And I left you there.

You eventually crawled into the bedroom to watch mindless cartoons.

That was my day. All I wanted was to spend time visiting your mom at the hospital. Because she is dying.

December 1, 2017

Dear Thomas,

Yesterday was the most humiliating day of my life. Your dad went with us to the DMV to sign off that you lived at his address. We had your State ID within the hour.

Shortly after, Randall from the treatment center called. He asked if I could check you into treatment by two o'clock. It was ten in the morning, and he was requesting I deliver you in four hours ... *from another island.* That would be tough even if we were already on Oʻahu. Randall confirmed he would pick you up at the Honolulu airport, but only if we landed in time to check you into rehab by two.

I hung up on Randall to book your Hawaiian Airline flight. I changed my original departure to be on the same flight—seated next to you—while simultaneously shoving your clothes and toiletries into a duffel bag, and packed my own clothes in a different bag. I didn't have a moment to hug your dad as he stood there watching all this happen. I threw our bags in the trunk and pushed you in the passenger seat.

"Bye!" I yelled to your dad as we raced out the driveway at 10:30.

"Good luck!" He knew our flight boarded at 11:30.

We were cutting it fucking close but I was determined.

Fuck! I still had to top off the gas tank for this rental car. *What happens if I don't?* I had never rented a car before. *How long is the process of returning the car?* I whipped into a gas station to top off, then back onto the road.

"Where are we going?" you asked. You were so fucked up you didn't even know what was happening.

I broke every speed limit. I roasted around every turn

and over every speed bump pulling into the rental agency. I barely opened the door when I screamed at the top of my lungs, "Can someone help me?" I popped the trunk and threw the keys at the first employee I saw. "Gotta go!" I had no idea if that was how you returned a rental car, but my guess was no.

I could see the shuttle bus for the TSA checkpoint but you were unable to stand on your own. I had my gym bag hanging from one shoulder with your duffle bag crisscrossed like a seatbelt over my opposite hip. And I had to carry you. You're almost a foot taller, and 220 pounds of drunk weight is a lot heavier than 220 pounds of sober weight.

"Hurry, babe! We cannot miss this shuttle!"

We barely made the shuttle. Seated across from us was a couple on their honeymoon. I was embarrassed but I had to ask the husband, "When we pull up to the curb, can you help?"

"Yeah, with what?"

"Just take his other arm."

"Okay."

They could see the distraught in my face.

The shuttle pulled up to the curb and I dressed myself with our bags. The honeymoon guy helped me hobble you toward the TSA line. I handed them our boarding passes and your temporary paper ID.

"I cannot accept a temporary ID."

"I need your supervisor, right now. This is *not* your problem. We are not going on vacation. *Look* at him. I am taking him to rehab. We have to get on this flight."

I could see the "oh my" in her face when she looked at you. Without hesitation, she called her supervisor. He came over, looked at the ID, at you, and understood.

"Can I get you a wheelchair?"

"No," you said.

"Yes please," I insisted.

"I need to use the bathroom," you said.

The agent directed us to the family bathroom. I had to hold you up because you couldn't stand on your own, let alone aim. You pissed all over the toilet, the wall, yourself. I would have held your dick for you but I was already holding both our bags, and you.

TSA was waiting outside with a wheelchair. They escorted us through a separate security line and patted us down, searched our bags, and wheeled you onto the plane. They had delayed the boarding process for us.

I texted Randall our arrival time and texted your dad, "We're on the plane."

You still didn't know what was happening.

"Where are we going?"

"We are going to O'ahu. You're going to rehab."

"Are you coming with me?"

"No. I have to go back to Maui. A guy named Randall will take you there."

You started crying and tried to hide your face on my chest. I wrapped my arms around you, kissed the top of your head.

"I love you. Everything's going to be okay."

After we landed, we were the last ones on the plane as we waited for your wheelchair. The crew wheeled you off. I thanked them for their compassion and assistance. We made our way down the elevator and waited on the curb for Randall.

"Who are we waiting for?"

"Randall. He is going to check you into the treatment center."

"Are you coming with me?"

"No, I have to go back to Maui." I explained again. "I have to work tomorrow."

Randall pulled up and opened the front door for you. I handed him your ID and $20 to buy you cigarettes.

I kissed you and said, "I love you."

"You're not coming with me?"

"No. I have to go back to Maui. I love you. We will talk soon."

I thanked Randall and blew you a kiss goodbye.

Holy shit. Did I really do it?

I delivered you to O'ahu and you're going to rehab.

Just as my heart rate returned to normal, my phone rang.

"Hey, what is wrong with him?" Randall asked, a loaded question.

"What do you mean?"

"Is he alright?"

"Randall, it's been a rough couple of days, and I just busted my ass rushing to get him to you by two o'clock."

"I don't think we can take him."

"You *have* to take him. You have no idea what we had to do to get him here. You know what? Call his dad. I have to catch my flight!"

I turned my phone off.

There's no fucking way everything I did was for nothing. As I waited another hour for my flight back to Maui, I sat in a bathroom stall and cried.

December 5, 2017

Dear Thomas,

I have been home for five days and I haven't heard from you. I am hoping no news means good news. I was in bed watching TV when I decided I was ready to confirm you were in treatment. I called your dad at 7:30 pm.

"Have you heard from Thomas?"

"No."

"Did he check into rehab?"

"I have no idea. I am sitting here with my dying wife."

"So, we have no idea where he is?"

"Correct."

I had deleted Randall's phone number because I didn't want to hear from him again. I googled treatment centers on O'ahu but so many are untraceable to remain discrete. With the phone numbers I found, some did not answer because it was almost eight o'clock, some would not confirm or deny if you were a patient, and some confirmed you weren't there.

So, I started calling hospitals. There are a lot of fucking hospitals on O'ahu. How was I supposed to guess where you would be? Queens was the fourth hospital I called.

"My boyfriend is missing. Do you have a patient with the last name Walker?"

"First name … Thomas?"

"Yes!"

"I will transfer you now."

"Thank you so much!"

"Hello?"

"What happened? Why are you in the hospital?"

"I don't know what I'm doing here, or how I got here. I'm scared and I'm alone in a strange city."

That's all I needed to hear.

I looked at the clock: 9:00 pm. I could make it. I booked a ticket on the last flight to Oʻahu, shoved a change of clothes in my backpack and raced to the airport.

On the way, I called my friend George to let him know I would be sleeping on his couch for the night. George was waiting for me at the Honolulu airport. He had recently moved into his new apartment and didn't even have a bed. As George was picking out bed sheets and shower curtains, I was processing my crazy life. Three hours ago, I was in bed in Maui. Now I'm at a fucking Wal-Mart in Honolulu shopping for an air mattress at midnight.

Dear Thomas,

George dropped me off at Queens Hospital as soon as visiting hours opened. I found your room and wasted no time cuddling with you in the hospital bed. I noticed your duffle bag was empty. Where did all the clothes I packed for you disappear? Your ID was missing, along with the $20 I gave Randall for cigarettes.

The doctor came in to prep you for the procedure you were about to experience. He explained that he would be putting a camera down your throat to take photos of your heart, making sure you didn't have any black spots from using heroin. You would be awake for this, but they'd give you a sedative to help relax because it would be uncomfortable. You looked uneasy and nervous, so I reminded you that I'd be right here when it was over.

The procedure went well and nothing serious showed up on your scans. It's unbelievable what you have done to your body. Like a cockroach, you won't die.

Your patient chart on the wall read, in big bold letters, IV DRUG USER.

Every staff member is aware you shoot meth and heroin, yet your IV bag consists of morphine and fentanyl. This is when it clicked with me that the opioid epidemic is fueled by money and politics. No one gives a shit about addicts.

I was holding back all day, but had to tell you one last thing.

"Things are not looking good with your mom. We have to face that she's not going to be with us much longer."

Dear Thomas,

Your mom is slipping. For days, you've been begging your dad to fly you back to Kona so you can say goodbye.

"I'm sorry son," he said, "You can hate me for the rest of your life, but you're not going to see your mom again."

He texted me to make sure I wouldn't buy you a plane ticket. Your mom is at home with hospice and there's morphine around the house. It is not the place for you to be. I reminded him that you'd lost your ID again, that you couldn't get on an airplane even if you wanted to.

"Call me," your dad texted while I was at work this morning, "it's about mom."

I had a feeling it was *the* call, so I hid in the parking lot.

"Barbara passed away peacefully in the middle of the night," he said, and those words ripped me apart.

It sucks we are all on different islands. Your dad is on the big island, your brother lives on Kaua'i, I am on Maui, and you are alone on O'ahu.

I called your hospital room as soon as I could.

"Hello."

"I just got off the phone with your dad. Are you okay?"

"It wasn't unexpected."

"I'm sorry I'm not there with you."

"I feel like this is my fault."

"This is not your fault," I said. "I won't deny you added stress and caused many sleepless nights for your mother the past year, but she had her own drinking problem. She did this to herself. This is not on you. Your mom loved you so fucking much."

Barbara was one feisty and strong independent woman.

She was a wife, a mother, a sister, a friend, and a phone call away. I feel lucky I got to know her. She loved me like a daughter and made me a part of the family. I won't bring myself to delete her phone number, her text messages, or the voicemails she left me. She will be missed and forever loved.

Dear Thomas,

You have spiraled since your mom passed. It has been difficult to get in touch with you since moving on from Queens Hospital to halfway houses. I haven't heard from you in almost four weeks. It's terrible always wondering where you are. I can only pray you're safe.

Last night was a horrible night. After twenty-six years of abuse, I finally ended my relationship with my dad. I lost count how many IPA's he drank at lunch. Then we went out for a sushi dinner with the rest of the family and he drank sake bombs. From there, we spent a couple hours at my godparents' house where he continued to blabber bullshit while polishing off a bottle of vodka.

I have been staying at my best friend Gabriella's house but I don't have my own car. I decided I would drop my dad off at home, drive myself to Gabriella's, and pick him up in the morning to take him to work with his truck. I have had an estranged relationship with my sister a few years now and my dad never accepted it. The entire drive home, he was screaming at me to reach out to her and repair our relationship. We pulled up to his gate while he was still ranting about my sister and me. He wondered why I hadn't cut the engine.

"Park here," he said.

"I told you I'm dropping you off. I'm driving to Gabriella's. I'll pick you up in the morning before work."

"Fuck you! This is my fucking truck! Park the fucking truck. We're not done talking."

I'm done. There is no reason why I need this abuse in my life. I am not ten years old anymore. I am done being spoken to and treated like this.

I threw the keys at him, got out of the truck and started walking on the side of Highway 1 between Cayucos and Morro Bay. I called Gabriella, hysterically crying.

"I need you to pick me up. I am fucking walking on the highway, in the dark, toward Morro Bay." I walked almost a mile before she found me in the bike lane.

Hours later, my dad texted, "Where did you go? How did I get home?"

"You're such a fucking drunk. I'm done with you. Me walking to Morro Bay on the highway at night is the last you'll ever see of me! You think you can treat me like that, and yell at me like that. *Fuck you!* And people think I'm weird for not drinking alcohol. I have never done anything to deserve your abuse. You're *dead* to me."

"Wow, that hits home. Thanks for your honesty. And fuck you too. You are a foul-mouthed liar. Good luck in your weird, bitter life. Peace out."

I already said my piece.

Who does he think I got my foul mouth from? Who is the cause behind my bitterness and anger?

I didn't sleep last night. I have been sick to my stomach all morning realizing what I am feeling is abandonment, even though I am the one cutting ties. He never physically abandoned me as a child, but he has emotionally abandoned me my entire life. It has taken me twenty-six years to figure that out.

I started crying when you sent me a Facebook message this afternoon. All month, I have tortured myself wondering where you were, what you were doing, and praying you were not dead in a ditch.

February 8, 2018

Dear Thomas,

I am relieved to hear you are staying at a Clean & Sober house. You got permission from the house manager to stay with me at the Sheraton Waikīkī. I was excited when you arrived. You looked good but I wasn't convinced you were sober.

I enjoyed our first night together. We splurged on an oceanfront dinner, spent the night catching up on sex and watching TV.

Yesterday, we spent the day at the infinity pool and then took an afternoon nap. I woke up at five o'clock remembering it was my last night with you. I woke you up so we could get dinner and continue making memories together. Then you stormed out of the hotel room and lit a cigarette in the hallway on your way to the elevator.

I ran after you screaming, "What the fuck are you doing?" I grabbed the cigarette and put it out in the elevator. We were staying at the Sheraton Waikīkī because of my benefits, which could be taken away in a second. I followed you to the lobby where you launched an empty plastic bottle across the room. Mortified, I extended the distance between us, not wanting anyone to think I was with you.

What the fuck is happening?

I chased you down the street.

"Thomas, Stop! I don't know when I get to see you next. I just want to have a nice dinner before I leave tomorrow."

While we waited for our food that night, you got up to use the restroom. I saw you pay the bartender a visit on the other side of the restaurant. You wanted to sneak in a few shots of vodka. I am not stupid, Thomas. Why not just order shots to the table? If you were afraid of disappointing me, we were way past that.

I didn't want you going back to the hotel with me. Our Uber driver dropped you off first. I rolled my eyes when I realized the Clean & Sober house shares a driveway with a liquor store.

The same driver dropped me off at the Sheraton. I was picking up the bathroom towels off the floor when a handful of vodka shooters fell out. I *knew* you weren't sober.

I enjoyed a bubble bath in silence, watched a chick flick, and fell asleep in the middle of the king-size mattress. I woke up this morning to messages from you:

"I love you. Can I see you today?"

"Last night was overwhelming for me and that is not how I want to spend my limited time with you. Please let today be a good day."

I rented a car to pick you up, and met the house manager and your roommates.

"You match," one said.

In other words, we make a cute couple.

You slept the entire drive to Waimea Bay, and as soon as I scored a parking spot, you woke up and said, "You didn't stop for beer?"

"No, I didn't."

"We need to go to the store."

"No, we don't."

"Babe, I need a beer."

"You can't enjoy one hour at the beach without a beer?"

"Take me to get a beer."

"We just got here. I'm *not* giving up this spot."

I got out of the car with my beach towel but you weren't going to the beach to spend time with me without a drink.

"I can't believe you didn't stop at the store on our way here."

"Seriously? Fuck you, Thomas. I fucking hate you right now. You are so ridiculous." I slammed the car door as I got back in the driver's seat. "All I wanted was to have a day at the beach without any drama."

You had nothing to say, you selfish prick.

I went inside the gas station while you sat in the car. I hope I bruised your dick when I dropped the six-pack on your lap.

We made it back to Waimea Bay where I got an hour of sun. It's fucked up that the only time I get to relax is when you sit in silence sipping on your beer.

Dear Thomas,

I had a strange dream last night. We were in a dark dungeon-looking hospital. I was trying to run to your room, but I kept slipping in my socks. I caught word that you'd left without being discharged, something you've done many times in the past, including escaping ICU. My friend was advising me not to go after you. You came back to the hospital, and we drove away together. You had detoxed but as soon as we hit the road you asked me to stop and buy you a beer (typical). I told you I was done with that shit, so I abandoned you at a Jack in the Box in Los Angeles (so specific). I woke up thinking, *What the fuck was that about?* I'd tell you about it, but I haven't heard from you in over a month.

Your dad texted: "I finally heard from Thomas. He is at OCCC."

"Oʻahu Community Correctional Center?"

"Yes."

"We can finally sleep better at night."

I have known a long time that jail is the only way you were going to get sober.

Dear Thomas,

At the start of this year, I stepped on a scale and was mortified: 168 pounds. I looked in the mirror and stared at my 5'2" frame of blubber. I don't recognize myself anymore. I hate my body so much. How did I let myself go so far?

I have been skinny my entire life so losing weight is something I have never had to do. A friend introduced the 21 Day Fix workouts to me, which are only thirty minutes long, and I started meal-prepping with colored containers. I am proud to share with you that I lost nine pounds in my first twenty-one days! I am repeating the process and starting to notice a difference in photos, especially in my face. It feels so good to release this fat and get healthy.

I am on Oʻahu today trying on bridesmaids' dresses. The lady trying to zip my dress said I needed to go up a size. I told her no. I have lost twelve pounds already and I plan to continue losing weight before Piper's wedding in August.

I was eating a salad inside the airport when my phone rang from an unknown caller. I don't normally answer unknown numbers, but I was hopeful it would be you.

An automatic recording. I realized it was a prompt to accept your call and got so excited. After almost two minutes of silence, I finally heard you say, "*Baby?*"

Then it hit me.

This was the first time in two years I heard your voice *sober*. It had been so long since I knew what sobriety sounded like in your voice.

"Oh my god, I am so happy to hear from you!"

"I'm happy to hear your voice."

"How are you?"

"I'm okay. It was rough the first couple weeks."

I laughed, then said, "Yeah, how was that detox?"

"I'm glad it's over."

"I'm on O'ahu. Piper and I were dress-shopping and about to fly back to Maui."

"I wish I could have seen you."

"Me too, babe. Me too."

May 9, 2018

Dear Thomas,

I love hearing from you on a regular basis. Almost every night at 8:00 pm you call me, and we get to speak for exactly fifteen minutes. If I don't get a call from you, it's because you called your dad, and you're only allowed one call per day. He and I always text each other to let the other know you love them. It's nice you have opened up about the events that landed you in jail, which hopefully we can laugh about some day. During our fifteen-minute phone call, you shared with me:

"I was kicked out of the Clean & Sober living house because the knuckleheads running the place realized I wasn't sober. I wandered the streets of Oʻahu for two weeks without a phone, and not eating because I lost my EBT card and ID, *again*.

"At the end of February, I took a metal lid off a trash can and threw it through a store window to break inside. A nearby construction crew heard the alarms going off. One of the workers tackled me to the ground after I tried escaping with a handful of wine bottles. I threw a few punches and wine bottles before he pinned me down. After the cops put me in the backseat, they sent an additional message by blasting my face with pepper spray. I called my dad after spending two weeks detoxing in my cell.

"It's hard to have conversations or relate to anyone inside here. Everyone is walking around, puffing their chest, aspiring to be the bigger badass. I'm surrounded by a bunch of male turkeys walking around with their big feathers fanned out. I spend my days playing card games and exercising. I've had plenty of time to think, pray, and read. I believe

I have gotten a lot wiser. I have come to know two things: one, I want nothing more than to stay sober, and two, I want to spend that time with you.

"I wish there is something I could do to right all the wrongs I have done to you, and for all the nights I have kept you up worrying. I guess I can start with an apology. Danyelle, I apologize from the bottom of my heart for everything I have done. I am so very sorry. I wish I could take it all back. I can say that it will never happen again, but actions speak louder than words. I cannot wait to show you a much brighter, happier, and joyful future. I am so thankful you haven't given up on me and that you've always been there. What a trooper you have been, and still are! I miss you so damn much. I squeeze my pillow and pretend I'm sleeping next to you all the time.

"Sitting in this jail cell is the last place on earth I want to be right now. But when I take a deep breath and really think about it, going to jail has gotten me sober. Something I've been trying to do but found impossible for the last two and a half years. So getting arrested has been a blessing."

Dear Thomas,

I woke up on your 33rd birthday to get ready to go to jail. Such a weird thing for me to write. I called ahead of time to confirm where the entrance was and how to enter.

"I don't think we're supposed to drive through the gate," I told my Uber driver.

"That looks like the door right there."

"Stop. I don't think you're allowed to go any farther. I'll get out here, but make an immediate U-turn right here," I said, pointing, and then thanked him for the ride.

As I was approaching the door to check in, a guard behind me yelled, "Hey, you better get that car out of here!" My Uber driver didn't go where I advised him to go.

"That's not my car."

"Get that car out of here!"

"Sir, it's an Uber. I can't control where they drive."

"You want to lose your visit?!"

What the fuck is he not understanding?

"Sir, it is an Uber. I don't give a fuck what happens to them."

He got in my face as I was trying to check in and yelled, "You're going to lose your visit then!"

There's something about *haole* men who speak with a thicker *pidgin* accent than the average local Hawai'ian. They are mean and intimidating as fuck.

"No! I am not losing my visit. I just flew here from another island."

He looked at the other officer and demanded, "Take her visit away!"

The man behind the counter saw the tears in my eyes

and shooed the asshole away.

"I'll need to see your ID. Who are you visiting?"

"My boyfriend. Last name Walker." I started crying. "I'm sorry. Can I use the bathroom? I need a moment."

I pulled myself together and was provided a locker. The nice guard gave me a map with a red line to follow, which would lead me to the visitor's waiting room.

That's it, a red line? No escort? In a correctional facility?

I walked through the courtyard where inmates play handball. There were a couple inmates out and about. I assumed these were the nonviolent offenders.

"Hey, you're Thomas's girlfriend."

What the fuck?

Who the fuck is this guy? Maybe he's seen a photo of me that I sent you.

"Yes. Today is his birthday. That's why I'm here."

He was nice and showed me where the red line continued. As I walked down the final hallway, more inmates were cleaning the floors and the walls.

I found the waiting room and checked in with another guard. He told me he would call me when you were at the window. The guard waved for me to approach.

I smiled when I saw you.

"Hi, baby."

"Hi, how are you?" you said, smiling back.

You had no idea what I had gone through, mentally and emotionally, just to get to this window to tell you 'Happy Birthday' in that ugly dark-green jumpsuit.

"I'm sorry, I'm a little shaken. This is my first time going through this process to visit and one of the guards was a total fucking prick."

"I'm sorry, baby. Yeah, these guys are assholes. It's their job."

You looked good and I wished I could hug you. I was hoping our visit would be at a table in a large room, like what you see in the movies. Not this. We were separated by shitty double-pane plastic windows. They were scratched up, dark, and foggy. And it was hard to hear each other, so we basically had to yell through the windows. Other visitors next to me were doing the same, yelling through the windows, everyone talking over each other.

Where are the phones? Another prop we only see in the movies?

I had sent messages to friends, family members, and loved ones, reminding them your birthday was coming up. I requested they send you a letter by May 24th so it would arrive on time. I wanted to make your birthday as special as possible and hoped you would feel the love. I imagined it would help pass the time, considering you wouldn't be home for a while. I asked everyone to wish you a happy birthday, to let you know about all the things going on in their lives, and to remind you of one of their best memories they created with you.

I have no idea who followed through, but you said you received over ten letters and the guy who drops the mail off at the cell doors had never seen anyone receive so many at one time. I was so happy to hear that!

As your present, I put $50 into your commissary so you can buy all the ramen, crackers, and cookies you want for your birthday.

We only had thirty minutes to visit. I was happy and grateful to see you, yet I was emotionally drained after walking out those jail doors.

June 28, 2018

Dear Thomas,

Last night during our regular call you let me know you'd be standing in front of a judge today. I just got off the phone with you and you're going to be released this coming Tuesday, July 2nd. How exciting! You also lined up a treatment center, but they won't have an available bed until after the holiday.

I can fly to O'ahu after work on Tuesday and we can spend a few days together before you check into treatment. I have a good feeling about this because today you are four months sober. Jail has saved your life *and* your liver.

I have vacation hours I need to use, so I can stay on O'ahu through Sunday night. I booked an Airbnb, a rental car, and my round trip airfare. $1,500. This is the most money I have ever spent for island-hopping, but it will be worth it. I am looking forward to spending 4th of July with you and making new memories together.

Dear Thomas,

July 2nd is *Monday*, not Tuesday. How did we mess up the dates? How many other inmates has this judge released a day earlier than their families expected? I already booked a place for Tuesday through Sunday, and I am unable to take another day off work to arrive a night earlier. This is so frustrating. I'm surprised at myself. I'm an organized perfectionist who never mixes up dates, calendars, or to-do lists.

I received a notification on my phone that you were released on probation at 9:39 am. You don't have a phone, so I had no way of getting ahold of you until you called from a stranger's number five hours after your release.

"Where am I supposed to go?" you said. "I have no money. My dad tried to rent me a hotel room but they wouldn't give me a key because I don't have an ID."

"We'll figure it out."

"I'm scared, I'm in a strange city, and I don't want to drink."

"I don't want you to drink either. Why don't you go to an AA meeting? I guarantee you'll meet someone positive and you can sleep on their couch tonight."

"I don't know where an AA meeting would be here."

"I'll find one for you, just give me a few minutes."

You scoffed and said, "I'll call you tomorrow."

"No, you will call me today, in an hour. I'll find you a place to sleep until I get there. You better call me back in an hour."

I texted some of your AA friends on Maui: "Do you know anyone on O'ahu?"

In a matter of forty minutes, I found you three places

to sleep. I couldn't wait for you to call back so I could give you the good news, but you never did.

And now it's late, and you still haven't called.

Where are you?

What are you doing?

Who are you with?

July 3, 2018

Dear Thomas,

I did not get one minute of sleep last night. Every possible scenario has gone through my head. I finally got a phone call from a random number two hours before my flight.

"Where the fuck have you been?"

"I don't have a phone," you said. "I slept on a bench."

"I found three places for you to sleep last night."

"I'm sorry. I should have called you back. That would have been nicer than sleeping on a bench."

"Have you been drinking?"

"No, I have not been drinking."

"Where are you?"

"Hanging out with people I met at the beach, in front of the Aston."

"Meet me at the Honolulu Zoo entrance at 6:30."

Your voice sounded different. Not the voice I'd been listening to on the prison phone the past four months.

Traffic in Honolulu was terrible but that's not what was causing my anxiety. I tried taking slow deep breaths, convinced you started drinking as soon as you hung up the phone yesterday and that was why you never called back.

I looped around the parking lot but you were nowhere in sight. After paying for parking to search for you on foot, I walked up and down the parking lot and around the giant banyan tree outside the entrance. I checked every park bench, looked across the park, and started walking up the street when I asked myself, *Where am I even looking?*

I walked around for twenty minutes in a city with over a million residents. That doesn't include the hundreds of thousands of visitors.

I couldn't imagine you sitting on the sandy beach, but fuck it, I checked. You said you were in front of the Aston, so I walked through their lobby and crossed the street.

Where are you, Thomas?

I could have aimlessly walked up and down Waikīkī all night.

Why are you doing this to me?

I didn't know what you were wearing so I backtracked and started searching for tattoos and spotted your right arm sleeve. You were sitting at a picnic table with people, smiling, laughing, smoking a cigarette. I snuck up behind a pillar because I wanted to surprise you. I was relieved to have found you but that quickly died. You were slamming a bottle of vodka.

I walked up to you, not smiling. As soon as you recognized me, you smiled like nothing in this twisted fucked up world mattered.

"Baby!"

"You're drunk."

"*Baby* …"

"Why am I here, Thomas? Why am I here?"

"Baby, I love you."

You're homeless friends were trying to make conversation with me but I blatantly ignored them.

Why the fuck did I come here?

I turned around to walk away, done with you.

You whimpered behind me, "Baby. Baby." You caught up to me and put your hand on my shoulder, and I turned around and looked into that sad face.

"Why are you walking so slow?"

"I have blisters from these prison shoes. They didn't give me socks."

"I am not doing this on the street in front of a million

families on vacation. If you want to talk, come to the banyan tree where there are much fewer people."

I couldn't stop crying. I had dropped $1,500 on a weekend you destroyed before it even started.

"I'm leaving you here at this banyan tree. You're not coming with me. I'm not spending another *minute* of my life catering to this shit."

"Baby, I know you're mad—"

"What the fuck is wrong with you? You were sober for *four months*. You detoxed *in jail*. The hardest part was over!"

"I'm going to rehab," you said, "but tomorrow is the 4th of July so we don't know if there's a bed for me until Thursday."

I shook my head.

"Baby," you said, "I got into rehab! We just have to wait a couple days."

Two days. Two days you'll be in rehab.

"Let's go."

You followed me to the car but kept stopping to hold me and cry on my shoulder. At this moment, I didn't want to be in your arms. I wanted to eat, shower, and sleep.

Dear Thomas,

Last night wasn't terrible. You didn't bother me to get you alcohol. We showered and went straight to bed, but we were watching a movie this morning when you optimistically asked me to drive to the store and buy you a beer.

"No!"

"Please, just one, I promise I only need one to feel better."

"No! It's never *just one*. I am not doing this. You're going to rehab. I don't give a fuck if the detox sucks. You were four months sober the other day. The worst part was already over. You did this to yourself."

"Baby, please. I swear, I am going to rehab. I just need to get through today."

"No!"

You spent the next thirty minutes desperately pleading and begging. It was unbearable. I would rather be in a room with ten screaming toddlers.

I went to the bathroom and you kicked in the door. You got down on your knees and begged while I was sitting on the toilet.

"Can I get some fucking privacy?"

"Just tell me we can get a beer and you can have your privacy."

"Thomas, get the fuck out! Shut the fucking door!"

"And then you'll take me to get a beer?"

"Get out!"

"And then we will go get a beer?"

"Oh my god! Get the fuck away from me! Now!"

"Baby, just tell me we will go to the store and I'll close the door."

"Yes! Fuck you! Are you fucking happy? Shut the fucking door!"

"You promise, you swear? I'll get the keys."

Fuck me.

We drove to the store and of course we didn't get one beer. You made sure you were stocked for the next twelve hours. I should have kicked you out on the street, but I was still holding onto the hope you would go to rehab.

All I wanted was to go to the beach today, but you would rather drink, sleep, and watch cartoons. But I kept one promise to myself and that was to see the fireworks.

We parked at Ala Moana as the sun was setting. You stopped inside the ABC Store to buy a beer, but also to steal a bottle of vodka. You weren't concerned about seeing the fireworks, or me seeing the fireworks. Fifteen minutes of joy wasn't a priority of yours. Sitting on the curb, I watched fireworks from afar while you drank away this memory.

While sitting in traffic, exiting the parking garage, the song "Meant to Be" by Bebe Rexha came on the radio. You turned up the volume, looked at me, and smiled.

"This is such a good song!"

You started singing at the top of your lungs. This would have been a sweet gesture sober. You were trying to make me smile but I was overwhelmed by your drunkenness. And if I smiled or enjoyed this moment, it made your alcoholic behavior acceptable.

I was crying so hard by the time we made it back to the Airbnb that I was shaking and hyperventilating. It crossed my mind to admit myself into the hospital for panic. You rubbed my back to "comfort me" while swigging vodka.

Why was tonight's stressful episode so much different than the times before? I guess I used to have momentum. In the past two years, I got used to the drama, the chaos, being there when you needed me, or when your mom begged me to jump at the first sign of trouble. I haven't had to do any of that since I flew you to Oʻahu last November. I had an eight-month break from playing superhero. I caught up on sleep while you were safe in jail for four months. I lost that momentum, something I was happy to be rid of. I got off that pendulum and I mentally, emotionally, and physically could not get on that swing again.

You fell asleep holding onto the vodka like a toddler with their bottle. I tried to take it from you, but you woke up with a death grip.

You finally fell into a deep sleep, and I eventually was able to retrieve the bottle.

Where the fuck am I going to hide this?

There was only one place you won't look and that's the oven. I shoved the bottle in the far back corner and quietly returned to my side of the bed.

I went to bed extremely sad knowing I would be saying goodbye to you in the morning. I decided if you didn't check into rehab, I'd drop you off on the streets of Waikīkī with the homeless. I am not doing this anymore.

Dear Thomas,

I woke up to you screaming.

"Where is the vodka?!"

"I don't know."

"Seriously, where is my vodka?"

"You drank it."

"No, I didn't! Where did you put it?"

"I didn't take your fucking vodka, Thomas!"

"Baby, where did you hide it?"

You searched all the places I knew you would—under the bed, in my duffel bag, the closet, inside the fridge, under the sink, the pantry cupboards. You never checked the oven. I tried to ignore you but you're a persistent motherfucker and a sane person can only take so much. You made sure to push me until I retrieved "your precious" from the oven.

"The oven? Why was it in the oven?"

"Because you wouldn't look there, you fucking asshole!"

While you drank from the bottle, I called the treatment center and a woman named Alexia answered.

"My boyfriend was released from OCCC a few days ago and we've been waiting for a bed to come available."

"What's his name?"

"Thomas Walker."

"Yes, we have an available spot for him."

"What does he need to bring with him?"

"Just his clothes and toiletries."

"We'll be there in forty-five minutes."

We were halfway to Wahiawā when you said, "I don't want to go to rehab."

"You are going to rehab. That was the fucking deal."

"I'm not going."

"This is it. Either you go to rehab, or I am dropping you off in Waikīkī."

"Take me to Waikīkī."

"Are you fucking *kidding* me? Seriously, this has gone on too long. You're going to rehab. We are done with this. Me, your dad. We're done."

"Turn around."

"We're not turning around, Thomas. I love you. You're going to be okay."

As I parked outside the treatment center, you demanded I buy you a beer. Was the bottle of vodka you had for breakfast not satisfying enough? I walked to the front gate and noticed a group of men sitting in a circle, obviously working on their recovery.

"Hello? Excuse me?" A woman came to the door and I asked, "Are you Alexia? We spoke on the phone. My boyfriend is Thomas. He is in the car, anxious."

Alexia walked with me to the car. She was friendly and she wasn't stupid. It did not take long for her to recognize you were intoxicated.

"Baby, this is Alexia."

You didn't say anything or even look at her.

I pulled her aside and asked, "Could you say something to encourage him?"

"I don't think he wants to be here," she said. "He would not have shown up drunk if he wanted to be here."

"He *needs* to be here. He cannot live like this any longer."

Alexia and I walked toward the building. "I can tell you are a sweet, caring person, and you love him, but you need to take care of you and put yourself first. He is a grown man creating his own predicaments. He is not your problem."

You approached us at the front door of the sober house.

"Let's go," you said. "I want a beer."

"We are here. There is a bed available. Just walk inside."

"No, I don't want to be here."

"Yes, you do," I cried and tried to shove you through the front door where you could detox, recover, and have a safe residence. I begged the staff members, "Please say something to change his mind."

"Honey, he doesn't want to be here."

I collapsed and curled up on the sidewalk. The entire staff and sober residents were staring at me crying my eyes out. Traffic drove by with rubberneckers witnessing the scene.

I froze when I realized Jack in the Box was across the street. Was this a premonition from four months ago playing out? The dream about you escaping the hospital, me slipping because I was trying to run in socks, my friend advising me not to go after you? In that dream we drove away, but as soon as we hit the road you asked me to buy you a beer. I told you I was done with that shit, so I abandoned you at a Jack in the Box in Los Angeles, California.

That dream.

And here I was now, crying on the corner of California Avenue in Wahiawā, staring at a fucking Jack in the Box.

"I'm going to have to call his probation officer," someone said, "and report that he showed up here drunk."

Staring at the ground, I had nothing to say.

I didn't care anymore.

"Baby, let's go," you said, "she's gonna call my P.O. Take me to Waikīkī."

Unbelievable.

I sat in the car in silence.

"Baby, are you gonna start the car?"

"Shut. Up."

I looked at you in disbelief and called your dad.

"I drove your son to rehab but he refused to go."

"Are you kidding me?"

"No. I'm dropping him off in Waikīkī with the homeless."

"I support your decision," he said without hesitation. "I am so, so sorry."

Your dad and I have become close this year. He's always supported me and never argues. He knows what needs to be done and that includes walking away from you.

If your mom were alive, she would be begging me to not drop you off with the homeless. She would send me money to rent a hotel room and buy you more beer to make you comfortable and continue to try and "fix" this broken part of you that can't be fixed.

You slept the entire drive back to Waikīkī. I pulled up to the curb outside the Aston where I found you two days ago.

"You can get out here."

"Can I get a beer first?"

"You can go steal a beer if you want one so bad."

"Baby, let's get beer and cuddle and watch Netflix."

"Get out of my car, Thomas. I am not doing this anymore. I told you if you weren't going to rehab, I was dropping you off in Waikīkī. Now get the fuck out!"

"Baby, c'mon—"

"Get out!"

You did and slammed the door.

I watched you walk away in the review mirror before I drove off. I called your dad again. He couldn't understand me because I was choking from crying so hard.

"I screamed at him to get the fuck out of my car. It was horrible. No apology, no hug, no goodbye, no I love you …"

"He didn't even say goodbye?"

"No. What if that's the last time I ever see him alive?"

"I'm so sorry, Dani. You had to do it. You have to save yourself. I support your decision."

"I feel horrible. I don't want him to die."

"I don't either, but he's sick. Only he can help himself."

Choosing to be done with you was the hardest thing I have ever had to do. Anyone who doesn't understand my decision or this pain should consider themselves lucky.

I called your probation officer next.

"He refused to go to rehab so he is back on the streets. He has no money so he will probably get picked up for stealing, so you might as well put a warrant out for his arrest."

"There is nothing I can do, unless he fails to show up for his drug screening."

"He is going to die if he doesn't go back to jail. You'll save his life by arresting him sooner rather than later."

Then I called your friend, Charly. She works at the rehab you went to in Texas a couple years back. I was already crying when she answered the phone.

"Oh my god. Oh my god. Is he …? Is this the call? Is he dead?"

"No!"

"Oh my god. You fucking scared me. What's going on?"

I caught her up on everything. She had no words. She was in as much disbelief as me. Her heart hurt for me.

"You have to be done with him," she said. "You're going to kill yourself constantly trying to save his life."

Dear Thomas,

Yesterday was my first day back at work and my boss informed me that I had won a recognition award for going above and beyond for the company.

"The managers are having lunch at the villa property. Are you up to receive your award in front of the team?"

I shook my head. "I do not feel good at all."

The one time I win an award at work and being recognized for something I worked so hard for—you took that experience away from me.

I had a climbing fever. By the time I got home, I could barely keep my head up. I collapsed onto my bed. I have never felt scared from being sick. I debated going to the emergency room.

I called my friend Ross who works down the street. I had zero energy to speak.

"I don't feel good."

"Hello? Are you there?"

"I don't feel good," I could barely manage.

"Are you okay?" He hung up and ran to my house and not much later kicked in the door. "What's happening?"

He and my roommates put bags of ice on top of me to help break the fever. I lay there for several hours under melted ice bags.

Stress can kill you.

It almost killed me, after you shattered my heart.

Dear Thomas,

I received two collect calls from you this week. Each twenty-minute phone call cost me $21.75. You were drunk, hungry, dirty, tired, and hopeless. I hope the only thing you wanted out of those phone calls was the sound of my voice because I am done hopping on flights to make you feel more comfortable. You had the red carpet rolled out for you to get into treatment and you stomped on it with your crusty feet.

Today, I received a notification that you have "returned to custody" and I laughed.

I hope you enjoyed your three-week vacation drinking on the streets. You belong in jail. Your dad texted me that he got the same notification.

Looks like we both get to sleep tonight.

July 31, 2018

Dear Thomas,

I called your dad on his birthday last Friday. He told me you would be calling.

"No!" I told him. "I am *done*."

"I know you're done, but he needs to face what he has done and apologize to you."

Yes, you needed to own up to your bullshit and make amends to me, but I didn't want to talk to you. I didn't want to speak to you ever again.

I am flying to Colorado next week for Piper's wedding. I have been at the salon for five hours getting my hair extensions sewn in. I warned my stylist I might be getting a call.

It was eight o'clock on the dot when my phone rang, and the caller ID read "OCCC." My stylist noticed that I had started shaking. I answered and followed the prompts for a minute and forty seconds before hearing the background noise on your end.

"Hello?"

You hesitated, then said, "Hi."

"Hi," I said, unamused.

You whispered slowly, "It is taking everything in me right now to not cry because I cannot cry in this place."

"Take your time."

I know you heard the attitude in my voice.

"I am so sorry," you said, slow and quiet. "I know you probably hate me."

"I don't have anything to say to you. It is un-fucking-believable what you did, what you put me through. You were sober for four months, had treatment lined up, and then you decided to immediately get fucked up?"

"I don't know what's wrong with me, but I can't do this anymore. I am telling you … I am *done* with that shit, and if you don't give me another chance, I completely understand."

It was such an awkward fifteen-minute conversation.

What the fuck did you expect?

I hung up and my stylist said, "That's not done."

August 16, 2018

Dear Thomas,

You have no one else to call but your dad. I can't imagine what it's like to be sitting in jail and no one on the outside wants to hear from you. All your friends abandoned you. No one checks on you anymore. No one sends me or your dad messages asking for an update. They have all moved on with their lives without you. They make it look so easy.

You called while I was in Colorado and my friends snapped at me, saying, "You better not answer that." They had a right to react that way.

How many times can they hear me say *I'm done?*

I felt bad ignoring the call. I answered a few of your calls, but hid it from them. I didn't want to explain that I am holding onto a glimmer of hope.

Dear Thomas,

You planned to tell the judge that you wouldn't leave jail unless a treatment center was there to pick you up. An admirable plan. I'll believe it when you prove it.

When anyone violates probation, they go inside for thirty days and are then thrown back on the street. That's how it works. You were the only one who stood in front of the judge and asked to remain in jail. The judge had to clear their ears.

"You want to *remain* in custody?"

"Yes. I'm not from this island and don't have family here. I don't know anyone on Oʻahu. I don't have a job or a home to go to. And I don't trust myself in my own custody. I need to go to rehab. I want to go to a treatment center directly from OCCC. If you put me on the streets again, I'll be back in here in a matter of time."

The judge respected your request, and you were the only one sent back to your cell. All the other parolees went back to the streets. I was pleased by this notion of yours. It gives me hope you are serious about cleaning up the mess you've created these past two years.

October 27, 2018

Dear Thomas,

Your mom passed away over ten months ago and it's time to honor her. We wish you could have attended your mom's service, but not everything can be put on hold for you to put your life back together.

I flew to Kona on Friday and met your mom's sisters. One sister's voice sounds just like Barbara. It was tripping me out, like she was there.

The service was beautiful. We took three boats out of Kona harbor to spread her ashes. Your brother, aunts, and childhood friends all jumped in the water. I stayed aboard and scattered flower petals next to your crying dad, who poured her ashes into the ocean.

"It didn't have to be this way," he said, referring to her death being preventable if she had quit drinking sooner.

It broke my heart to hear him say that.

When everyone was back in the boats, the captains circled around the memorial. I started crying because I knew if you were here you would not have gotten back in the boat. I pictured you floating in her ashes, surrounded by flower petals. You two fought hard but loved hard. You were close with your mom. I'm sorry you didn't get to be here.

We ended the day with a dinner at the harbor. I listened to your brother and friends reminisce about your mom, sharing childhood stories. I also shared my memories of Barbara. I loved her so much, and she adored me. She thanked me all the time for loving you.

She loved how much I showed you my love.

November 5, 2018

Dear Thomas,

I didn't get to spend my birthday with you, but I was happy you called this time. You sent me a letter with a drawing inside, a sketch of a merman kissing his mermaid with his arms wrapped around her. It would make an outstanding tattoo! Whichever inmate you traded saltine crackers for the drawing is a talented artist.

I wish you could see how far I have come along with my weight-loss journey. I took a photo wearing my new birthday bikini and compared it to a photo from nine months ago. It's amazing to see the progress when putting the photos side by side. I absolutely hated myself nine months ago. I wasn't putting myself first, and instead dropping anything I was doing to be there for you. Losing over fifteen pounds has been one of my biggest accomplishments.

Looking good on the outside doesn't mean shit if I don't feel good on the inside. Since I started eating correctly, meal-prepping, and consistently working out, I sleep better, work better, and live better.

December 25, 2018

Dear Thomas,

December is always the most difficult month, financially. I paid my rent two weeks late and had no money left over to get me through the rest of the month. My credit cards are maxed out. I tried to buy groceries and put gas in my car, but my cards keep declining. I work so fucking hard but I'm struggling. I'm defeated. It's times like these I wish you were here to pick up the slack. All my friends are in relationships. They all have partners that meet them halfway. I do everything on my own.

I like my job, but I don't get paid enough. I have been working at a call center from 7:00 am to 3:00 pm, then I change my clothes in my car, slam some food, and work my new job at The Luxury Hotel from 4:00 pm to 9:00 pm. I do this four nights a week. I typically work sixty hours but this week I worked seventy. And today is Christmas and I worked fourteen hours.

Our friend Meeka told me to stop by her house on my way home. She wanted to exchange gifts. I asked her if we could do it another day, but she insisted. She handed me a card and a small box and said it was from you.

You got me a Christmas present, *from jail?*

Obviously, I was never expecting anything from you. I opened the box and inside was a beautiful silver, hammered heart-shaped pendant with two soft-pink beads on each side. This is the sweetest thing you have ever done for me, and it brought tears to my eyes. I needed this. Not the gift itself, but that you thought of me.

I missed a few of your calls this week because I have been at work. If I don't have a hotel guest in front of me I can take your calls in the bathroom, but if I have someone in front of me I miss the call and cry because I cherish those minutes.

I love you so much, Thomas.

Christmas was your mom's favorite holiday. All she wanted was for us to be together but that didn't happen this year. I'm on Maui, your dad is on the big island, your brother and his wife are on Kaua'i, and you are in jail on O'ahu.

This would not have been her ideal Christmas.

January 17, 2019

Dear Thomas,

Last night on the phone you said you were feeling sad and hopeless. You miss your friends, miss freediving, and miss your life before you relapsed. You have been in jail (this time) for almost six months, and have been patiently waiting to be picked up from a treatment center, but there is no way of telling when that will happen.

I was going to sleep in today, but I awoke to my phone vibrating at 7:30. The caller ID read "OCCC." You never call in the morning.

"Hello?"

"Hey! Sand Island is here to pick me up."

"What?"

"Yeah, I'm getting out today."

"Oh my god, babe! You were so sad last night because we didn't know when you were going to move to rehab."

"I know. Let my dad know I'm going to Sand Island."

"I'm going to call him right now. I love you!"

"I love you! Muah!"

It's happening. It's finally fucking happening.

February 19, 2019

Dear Thomas,

The day Sand Island picked you up from OCCC, I mailed you clothes and toiletries. You are not allowed phone calls or letters the first thirty days, and I am not allowed to visit you until ninety, but you surprised me with a call on Valentine's Day. Your counselor was nice to let you use his phone and make that day special for me.

I need to get my debt and expenses under control, so I started driving Lyft. Between rides, I read *Total Money Makeover* by Dave Ramsey. I wrote down my monthly and annual expenses and realized I have been spending $750 a year on an unnecessary storage unit. I am obsessed with Marie Kondo's Netflix series as well, so I have been purging, donating, selling, and throwing everything away. I am already saving money.

There is also drama between me, human relations, and the corporate manager at the call center about working at The Luxury Hotel. I was still working sixty hours a week between jobs but I gave my two weeks' notice at the call center yesterday, which didn't go over well. Thirty minutes before my shift ended, my boss sent me a message to come to his office.

"Today is your last day working for us," he said.

"No, it's not."

"Yes, it is."

"You're really going to do this to me?"

I only needed one more shift to qualify for my bonus, and planned to spend the next two weeks emailing my clients and introducing them to their new personal concierge.

"We will figure it out," he said.

"No, you won't. I am the most organized person in this office."

"I know you are. You're one of the best team members, and I wish I could pay you more. If I could give you the title of a senior position, I would."

I had quit on paper, but the company decided to fire me instead. It hurt because I consider my boss (now ex-boss) a friend, and I knew he didn't want to do this to me. It was his corporate douchebag boss. He was also supposed to have a second manager in the room when firing someone, which is why I didn't suspect anything when I first sat down. While things were heated, he turned to his computer to message another manager to join us. He probably thought I was going to beat him with the stapler based on my tone. At one point, he tried to interrupt my anger by letting me know I had won an award.

"What are you talking about?"

"You were nominated by your coworkers as the most supportive and valuable team member. We're having a ceremony this Friday and you're supposed to be there."

"Obviously, that is not happening. Do you have a box?"
"What?"

"Do you have a box so I can pack my desk?"

"Why don't you come back later after everyone has gone home."

"Oh no, we're doing this right now."

I want everyone to see this.

"Can I have the password to your computer, email, and voicemail?" he asked, handing me a banker box. I gave him the 'you fucking kidding me?' look.

He had already stated they'd figure it out.

I went to my desk and pulled out everything from the drawers, not saying a word. The room silent. Eyes on me. Everyone thinking, *What the fuck's happening?* Everyone looking over their cubicle windows. I didn't make eye contact with anyone and walked right out the door. And you better believe I didn't clock out. I was escorted out by the manager below him.

Such a joke.

The cherry on top was that it was absolutely pissing rain. I stood under the covered parking lot with my banker box full of crap. Like a scene from a bad movie. It was also the only day I had parked at the top of the hill, so I was soaking wet by the time I got to my car.

I then called The Luxury Hotel and told them I'd be available full-time for them and only them. They asked if I wanted a couple days off because of what happened, which would have been nice, but I couldn't afford a day off.

I am no joke broke, but I guess shit like this has to happen so the shift can happen.

Dear Thomas,

You have tried to explain this disease to me in the past, and I have always wanted to understand, but for some reason I struggled until I opened today's letter from you:

> I would really like you to get a better understanding of this whole situation. The American Medical Association declared that alcoholism was a disease in the 1950's, yet almost seventy years later, we still find ourselves asking questions like, 'Why does he behave like this?' 'Why can't he control his liquor?' 'Why can't he have just one or two?' 'Why does he always go back to that first drink which will lead to ten?'
>
> Behind these observations is a world of ignorance and misunderstanding. If a person has the disease of cancer, Alzheimer's, or multiple sclerosis, all are sorry for them.
>
> But with the disease of alcoholism we see fierce resentment, frustration, fear, worry, horrible domestic situations, loss of trust, and most importantly the loss of hope. But you, my little angel, have not lost hope because you are still here.
>
> Alcoholism is the only disease you get yelled at for having.
>
> *It's also the only disease loved ones get yelled at for caring.*
>
> It's a disease of the mind and body, which I can abundantly confirm. The body of the alcoholic

has an allergic reaction to alcohol. To better explain this, I will use an example of someone who is allergic to shellfish. If they eat shellfish, the manifestation of the allergy would be a swollen tongue, face, and lips—something you'd notice physically. But with someone who is allergic to alcohol, the manifestation of the allergy is an actual physical craving for more of the same. The same goes for drugs. Therefore, if the alcoholic could stay away from the first drink, he would never trigger the allergy and get drunk.

So, here's where the alcoholic runs into the main problem—the mental obsession.

The mind of an alcoholic who is not drinking is restless, irritable, and discontent. When feeling this way, all he does is obsess on the ease of comfort that comes instantly by taking a few drinks. But after he drinks, he triggers the physical allergy and gets drunk every time.

You have seen me do this many times! Please, baby! Just one or two so I can feel better! Which I had every intention of doing, but once I took the first one, I triggered the allergy and could never stop. This cycle is repeated over and over. And I can't justify this behavior because I've known about this for a long time.

In summary, when I'm not using drugs or alcohol, I am always restless, irritable, and discontent. Alcohol and drugs are what I use to medicate myself, so I don't feel that way.

When we first met, I was still practicing spiritual principles every day. When I started experiencing material success, like a promotion at work and driving a brand new truck, I failed to see that it was because I was practicing these principles daily that I was experiencing success. I slowly stopped and started feeling restless, irritable, and discontent, leading me to take that first drink.

I want to encourage you to please ask me any questions you want and never think that any question you ask will ever change the way I feel about you. I am so lucky to have encountered such a beautiful person like you.

My last relapse did not just give me pain and misery, it taught me a wonderful life lesson, which is to make sure I do not forget what is important in this life. Things like family, love, spirit, and the development of the human soul. You are a huge part of that development, Danyelle. I love you so much!

Wow. Thank you, Thomas, for explaining the disease of alcoholism. In this letter you have described it perfectly. I finally understand. I finally fucking get it.

April 28, 2019

Dear Thomas,

You've been at Sand Island Treatment Center for more than ninety days, which means I finally get to visit you. Your counselor went over the rules and the schedule with me. Friday onsite dinner visits are from 4:30 pm to 7:30 pm. Saturdays, you get a pass to leave the facility with me from 12:00 pm to 7:30 pm. Sunday onsite lunch visits are from 11:00 am to 1:30 pm. I work weekends, so I have to request time off, which I can't do regularly.

Sand Island offers Wednesday visits, but they have a weird rule: I have to attend four Friday AA meetings with you before I am allowed to visit on Wednesdays. I don't understand the rule, and it could take an entire year for me to manage that. I thought about requesting four Fridays off in a row to bust it out, but I don't have money to fly to Oʻahu so often.

I flew to Oʻahu Thursday night and stayed at George's apartment again. I was scheduled to arrive at Sand Island Treatment Center for my drug test at four o' clock on Friday. My Uber driver asked where I was going, and I explained what I was doing on the island. He opened up and let me know his wife is also an addict and has been in recovery for years. He advised me to no longer pursue our relationship. But he must not know what true love is, and that makes me sad. For him to say "it's not worth it," must mean he's not in love with his wife.

A female employee escorted me to the office when I arrived, and then to the bathroom to watch me pee in a cup. Once confirmed negative, I waited for you.

We hadn't seen each other in ten months, not since I

had dropped you off in the streets of Waikīkī.

I was excited but nervous to see you.

You came around the corner and we both smiled. I could tell you were shy and nervous too, but also excited. Public display of affection is against the rules, so we quickly hugged and were escorted to our private visitors room where you kissed me. You kept your lips closed, and I knew why before you told me. Your dad told me a few weeks ago that one of your decayed front teeth had cracked while eating cereal.

"I chipped my tooth," you said, "it's so embarrassing."

"Don't be embarrassed. I should have knocked that tooth out a long time ago."

We laughed because it's true and talked about the craziness. Finally a sober conversation. I know you don't remember the details of everything you've put me through. But you know it was mayhem. You looked into my eyes and said two words you have said before but I had never felt: "I'm sorry."

Forgiveness is something I have always struggled with. It could be the Scorpio in me, but to me forgiveness means making all the horrible things you have done to me acceptable. I don't understand forgiveness. My dad is easily someone I will never forgive, but for some reason it's easy for me to forgive you.

"What do you want to do for work when you get back to Maui?" I asked.

"I was thinking about getting into air conditioning."

"That would be awesome. I'm sure there are plenty of companies you can choose from. Where do you plan on living? Do you want to get your own place and live with roommates?"

"I assumed I would move in with you," you said, which was nice to hear.

Then the bell rang, signifying dinner was ready.

I stayed in our visitors room, and when you brought back our meal, you also handed me a poem you had written called "Daydreaming."

> When I look up into a sunny sky
> I take a moment and close my eyes
> and as the sun beats down upon my face
> I suddenly smile as I picture your face
> up above into the sky
> both of us are flying high
> and as we land upon a distant cloud
> a little angel speaks out loud
> saying he was sent by God from above
> to tell us what we have is much more than just love
> saying we are among the very few
> to experience what others never do
> and as the little angel flies away
> I open my eyes to a sunny day

You writing me a love poem is the sweetest thing you have done for me.

It's comforting to know you feel the same way about our love being so rare.

I didn't want our visit to end but I knew that I would spend the following day with you. I was excited but couldn't stop thinking about all the possible ways you could fuck up our Saturday visit. It would be your first day in public and I couldn't help but think you were going to ask me for a beer and ruin everything.

Saturday morning, my Uber driver drove me to Sand Island to pick you up and then we rerouted to the movie theatre. I couldn't keep my hands off of you in the car but all I could think about was you fucking up this entire day.

We were standing in line at the concession stand when you noticed they served beer.

"They serve beer at movie theaters?"

"Yep."

Oh god, please don't ask for one.

"What the fuck?" you said. "The world is changing in strange ways."

I held my breath. Silence.

You ordered an energy drink at the counter.

Okay, I think we are making progress here.

We sat in our seats. You were excited because you hadn't done anything fun and relaxing in a couple years, not sober anyway. At one point during the movie, you got up to go to the bathroom. I held my breath again.

Oh god, this is your chance to fuck it up.

You could take a shot of alcohol in the bathroom or not come back at all. I had told myself if I wanted to be in this sober relationship, I had to trust you wholeheartedly. I would no longer babysit you.

You came back five minutes later, and I acknowledged that the rest of the day was going to be a good day. If you wanted to fuck up this day, you would have done so already.

You're going to be at Sand Island for the next two years, which means I have to wait another two years for you to come home so we can start our lives together. People have asked me if I am crazy … not to have left you. Two years is a long time but I plan on spending the rest of my life with you, which makes two years nothing. The few hours I spend with you are worth the thousand hours I spend without you.

Every relationship has its ups and downs, and we have survived the lowest lows, so I will wait to enjoy the highest highs.

Dear Thomas,

Your birthday is this Thursday, so I made sure to visit you this weekend. We drove to Lanikai Beach in Kailua to hike and swim. Before hiking, I figured you could use your first birthday present. You opened the gift bag in the car: Maui Jim sunglasses. They looked amazing on you, and you ended up needing them for the hike.

We spent the rest of the day relaxing at my Airbnb before I drove you back to Sand Island, where I gave you your second present: a custom love book.

I created avatars that looked like us and picked my favorite templates. One was a photo of my avatar wearing a light switch and yours switching it on.

"I love how you turn me on," it read.

The last page was a picture of us on top of a mountain.

"We've experienced heavy highs and heavy lows," it read. "No matter what, I love you from the bottom of my toes. I think about you every day. Even though we can't see each other or talk, I always say out loud, "I love you," every day. I will never give up on us because our love is deeper than the ocean. Basically, I kind of love being in love with you."

You closed the book and started crying.

It means a lot to me that you love your gifts and know how much I love you. I think back to when we first started seeing each other and you were against being in a relation-ship. You had been hurt before and I was determined to let you know you didn't have to be afraid to love again, that you would be missing out on unconditional love, and that I would never abandon you.

I love you so much.

People don't understand our love and my commitment to you, but I don't give a *fuck* what other people think. No matter how impossible, unattainable, or unimaginable something may seem, if it is *meant* to be, it *will* be.

September 8, 2019

Dear Thomas,

I flew to California last week to witness my best friend get married. A month before the wedding, my bridesmaid's dress didn't fit so I made the decision to crash diet. I lost fifteen pounds and eleven inches in four weeks! My dress was loose the day of the wedding.

It's crazy to think how much I used to hate my body. I have lost twenty-five pounds in the last eighteen months.

As we were getting pampered by an amazing team of hairstylists and make-up artists, I was surprised to get an unknown FaceTime call … from *you!*

You were recently approved to start working temporary jobs on the weekends and you called from one of your friend's phones. You have never seen me dolled up before and told me how beautiful I looked. You caught me on the perfect day. I was feeling beautiful in my own skin.

I flew to O'ahu after my trip to California so I could visit you three days in a row. I checked in at Sand Island for our Friday dinner visit. You surprised me and told me we were granted two full-day passes from 12:00 to 7:30 pm on Saturday and Sunday.

Yesterday, we watched stand-up comedy. You laughed so hard, and it was nice to hear. I hadn't heard you belly-laugh in a long time. A belly-laugh alone can reveal how sober someone is, not only in their bloodstream but their mind, body, and soul. And then we went out because you needed a new pack of cigarettes. I hate that you still smoke. You went into the gas station for a pack while I waited in the car. When you returned, the mood switched in a second.

"What the *fuck?*"

"What?"

I pointed at the drink in your hand.

"Babe, it's a Rockstar."

I couldn't breathe and my face fell in my hands. I broke down crying, traumatized. You had never seen me like that through sober eyes and felt terrible. I believe right then and there you realized the trauma you had put me through for so many years.

"Everything's okay," you said, putting your hand on my shoulder.

You started laughing, but I wasn't ready. I needed to let those tears fall.

Dear Thomas,

This weekend was our first overnight visit in seventeen months. You were working in Kapolei when I landed so I drove there to meet you for lunch. From there, I checked into my Airbnb in Waikīkī and headed to Sand Island. The office called ahead of time to let me know they were canceling visits because too many people inside the facility were sick, but they were generous and allowed me to pick you up so we could go out to dinner. After being there for almost a year, you have earned a lot more privileges.

At dinner you talked about switching jobs.

"The pest control company pays more," you said.

"I don't think that is a reason to switch jobs. If you want to work in air conditioning when you return to Maui, you should continue learning the trade with the HVAC company. You don't have bills, so what's more money going to get you?"

"I'm going into pest control."

You always do what you want to do, though, so you made the decision to leave the HVAC company and turned in the company cellphone. I like you having a phone, so we went to AT&T and I bought you a new one, then we went ice skating.

It was nice not having to rush back to Sand Island.

You were able to spend the night with me, something we haven't done in over a year, so I thought it would be a good time to have a conversation about our future, and to talk about something we'd never discussed before.

"Do you want kids … someday, I mean?"

"Absolutely. It's something I don't want to miss out on."

"We've never talked about it, because step one was you staying alive."

"Yeah, we can check that off the list."

I fell asleep before you, and when I woke up in the middle of the night I was shocked to find you sleeping. I hadn't seen you sleep in years.

All that time wreaking havoc, you never slept at decent hours. You would keep me up, or have me drive you to the emergency room late at night, or I'd wake up in the middle of the night and you'd be watching cartoons, smoking a cigarette outside, or be missing. To witness you sleeping so peacefully was the nicest thing about the weekend.

December 25, 2019

Dear Thomas,

Christmas finally fell on my scheduled day off, so we were able to spend Christmas Day together and celebrate several milestones, such as you being sober for 500 days, and finally giving up smoking.

It was pouring rain and you took me to one of the houses you've been working on. The place was beautiful, and it was cool to get a tour of someone else's empty boujie home.

We went upstairs to exchange gifts. I bought you a cellphone two weeks earlier so I didn't get you anything more extravagant. I got you several books and a fun deck of playing cards with sober quotes such as, "One Day at a Time" or "Progress Not Perfection" or "Let Go and Let God" or "Keep Coming Back" (not to mention I pay for all these trips for us to have quality time together). But what I really wanted to get you for Christmas is something you can't have inside Sand Island, so it will have to wait till next year.

I opened the present you gave me and inside was a small red box. Inside were two diamonds. I never had diamond earrings before and they are beautiful!

"Hi, baby," read a small handwritten note inside. "I love you so much and now that you have diamonds from me, I hope you know it means you're mine now, forever. Love, Thomas."

In that giant empty house, you took me inside the walk-in closet to undress me and put me on Santa's naughty list. All I wanted for Christmas is what I already got, and what I got can't be bought. *You.*

April 29, 2020

Dear Thomas,

It bugs me that I don't know when we will get to see each other again since the world is on lockdown with this pandemic. I haven't seen you since we had another overnight visit in February. We were at the waterpark when we started hearing rumors of a virus in China. I was going to visit you the weekend of March 21st, but the world shut down, canceling our plans.

My last day of work was March 18th. I never thought I'd see the day where both your dad and I are unemployed but *you* are still working. I have been scrimping and learning how to cook during this lock-down. I spend my days reading books about finance because *this* is the year I will pay off my debt. I am also exercising like crazy, doing two Beachbody workouts at sunrise, and walking four miles at sunset.

I have officially surpassed my goal to weigh 135 pounds. This morning I weighed in at 133! In the past twenty-six months, I have released thirty-five pounds. It has been quite the journey to get healthy. I can already tell a lot of other people's waistlines are expanding from the stay-at-home life. Everyone thought they were getting two weeks off work but it's already been six. I am taking this time in quarantine to self-love instead of self-destruct.

Dear Thomas,

I was upset I couldn't spend your 35th birthday with you due to travel restrictions. I know there isn't much we would be able to do, but being together is enough.

You have now moved on to the outpatient part of Sand Island's program and into a halfway house with some of the guys. I also changed my address this month.

Auntie Anne and her husband asked me to move into their home and be the property manager after they moved to California. They envision us to be the perfect team to take care of the property. I'll manage the rooms, tenants, and rent, while you take care of landscaping, maintenance, and repairs.

My friends Kaed and Taya moved in with me. The other bedrooms are empty, but I am searching for the perfect roommates. I'll make sure to not welcome lazy day-drinkers or party animals into our home. I don't want our kitchen to look like a minibar. I will be upfront and honest with every potential roommate about your recovery (discretely), and be conscious of avoiding any temptation in our home that might jeopardize your sobriety. I don't even keep Benadryl or NyQuil in the medicine cabinet.

I am waiting and counting down until the day you get to move into this beautiful home with me and our roommates.

Dear Thomas,

I am finally able to travel inter-island without having to quarantine. It's nice that I get to stay with you at the halfway house and you are driving a work truck. I am saving money not having to rent an Airbnb or rental car.

You warned me that your boss would try to convince me to move to Oʻahu after he invited us to the beach park barbeque. He wants to hold onto you as an employee forever, but you told him many times that we have our life on Maui and that's where we want to build our future. He offered us housing on Oʻahu, and a job for me. Even though he said he wasn't going to budge, I didn't feel bad telling him no.

Lately your boss has you doing more house projects than pest control. It was nice when you took me to one of his multi-million-dollar mansions yesterday. I have never walked through a property like that. We had the entire place to ourselves. You knew I'd enjoy tanning and swimming in the saltwater pool. It was relaxing and peaceful with no one around.

We didn't sleep there, but that would have been nice. Sharing your twin bed at the halfway house isn't comfortable. I am small, but you take up the entire bed. We'd fit perfectly if you'd spoon me, but you don't. You'd rather hug your pillow with your back to me, falling asleep to your stupid Adult Swim cartoons. I would rather sleep in darkness and in silence.

I sat up last night because I was uncomfortable, frustrated, and annoyed. I never snap at you (when you're clean and sober), and we never fight (when you're clean and sober), but I couldn't take the noise and told you to turn off the fucking TV so I could sleep. I love you, but this twin-size bed thing is not happening in our future.

My body is in the best shape it has ever been, which is why I wanted to hike today. I have spent the majority of the pandemic exercising, and after expressing that I wanted to hike Koko Head, you took me there. It's tough but rewarding with its view of Hanauma Bay and the rest of the island. Some steps were more than three feet high, so I had to get on my hands and knees to climb to the next, taking several stops to catch my breath. You kept pushing me to not stop, saying, "You can rest at the top."

And at the top I started crying, realizing the date: July 5th. The two-year anniversary of one of the worst days of my life. The day I drove you to Wahiawā, embarrassing myself in front of the treatment center, and then dropping you off with the homeless in Waikīkī.

I cried because the hike was hard as fuck, but I had survived harder, like the pain and agony you brought into my life when you were on a bender. I put on weight, lost my hair, wasted time and money, and lost myself. All because I wouldn't stop caring for you and loving you. The hike up Koko Head was difficult, but it has nothing on what you put me through and I am glad that time in our life is in the past.

Our future is bright, just like the view of Hanauma Bay.

Dear Thomas,

"I don't know what's going on," you said in a panic over the phone.

"What are you talking about?"

When you pulled into work, there were over forty FBI agents raiding the office. You kept driving and went to the mansion where you took me on the 4th of July and found more FBI agents there since they'd blown off the gate to the driveway.

I turned on the news to find your boss, or *former* boss, labeled as an organized "crime boss," like the mafia in New York or Chicago.

He's pleading guilty to seventeen felony charges, including kidnapping, murder-for-hire, racketeering, tax evasion, extortion, robbery, money laundering, and drug trafficking. The indictment even alleges he released the chemical chloropicrin into two different nightclubs to conceivably disperse anyone on the dance floor.

His arrest this morning happened after authorities executed raids across Oʻahu. The FBI raided the pest control office, his multi-million dollar homes, boats, and pricey cars. He had lent me one of those cars so I didn't have to rent one while visiting you.

The pest control business is a legitimate company, but it is said to have been used as a "headquarters" for planning criminal activities and fraudulently "employing" individuals engaged in acts of violence. The same pest control company where you work.

Apparently, this all stems from the disappearance of a young man in July 2016. Your boss's son died in a car accident but his best friend survived. Your boss is now accused of hiring associates to kidnap and murder that best friend. He is also accused of purchasing a boat to dispose of the body, which has not been found.

What the actual fuck? I've seen that boat on FaceTime, and there were times he sent you to the marina to clean it. FBI agents have been investigating him for years!

I just met him not even two weeks ago, and am confident they were watching us enjoy the mansion on the 4th of July weekend.

Let's pretend for a second that we *did* consider moving to O'ahu permanently. Let's pretend we took him up on his offer to live in one of his homes, *working* for him. We would have been getting groomed. What the fuck were our roles going to be in this alleged crime organization?

August 18, 2020

Dear Thomas,

Since your boss was arrested, you became unemployed for the first time during the pandemic. You spent the week catching up on Adult Swim cartoons and not putting effort into finding a job. You won't thrive collecting unemployment. And sitting around doing nothing isn't good for your sobriety.

I found an HVAC technician position for you on Craigslist. You need more experience if that is what you want to do as a career. It didn't take long to figure out how disorganized this guy was, so you came to the conclusion that if this idiot could manage a company with nonstop work, then you could own your own HVAC business.

You are a hard worker and like fixing air conditioning units. You used to fix them at the Lāhainā crack shack for drugs. Your former (now incarcerated) boss instilled confidence in you to take charge of projects and to not be afraid of trying new ideas.

"What do you think about opening our own company together?" you asked.

"You and me?" An exciting but nerve-wracking thought.

I come from a family of entrepreneurs. My grandparents owned their own pool-cleaning business, my dad owns his own screen-printing shop, my godparents own a roofing company, and all my uncles own their own businesses. I would be following in the footsteps of my blood by opening a small family-owned business with my significant other.

You know how organized and smart I am. You know I was born to run a company. You know this could only happen if I was on board.

"Let's do it."

Today I went hiking with girlfriends at Polipoli. It is nice and cool compared to Lāhainā. We hiked the Boundary Trail, which I would describe as a fairytale picture book. Whenever we turned a corner, we were in what felt like a different climate and enchanted scene. Polipoli is a magical place and it makes sense this would be the forest where I would get my creative juices flowing.

I will never forget this day because I came up with the name of our future business. It's cute, catchy, and to the point.

Dear Thomas,

The sun was setting in Lāhainā when I received a text: "Saw on Facebook that Uncle Glenn is gone! Don't know the details but apparently a head-on collision on a motorcycle? So sad right now. Going to bed. Sorry to give you the sad news. Love you."

I read the message again but stopped at 'Uncle Glenn is gone!'

No. There's no fucking way.

I collapsed, holding my stomach. The thought of him passing was a fear of mine my entire life. There was no way this was happening now.

Crying hysterically, I FaceTime'd Gabriella. I scared her because I couldn't get the words out and it was obvious something terrible had happened. Her first assumption was you, another relapse or overdose. She played the guessing game until I could spit it out.

"My Uncle Glenn is gone, forever."

I called my mom: no answer.

I called my godmother: no answer.

They probably didn't know, I assumed, because they were hosting my sister's baby shower, which I was missing. I miss a lot of family events on the mainland—the price of living in paradise.

9:30 pm in California and no one answered.

"Someone call me!"

My godmother finally did. She knew. She was the first. She got the call during the baby shower and had to hold it together the entire party. And she was the one hosting the shower. Uncle Glenn had called her Friday night, confirming he was going to be surprising my sister at the party. "He went out to buy a gift for her," she said, "when he collided head-on into a highway patrol vehicle."

When the party ended, my godmother told my parents what had happened, and they all decided they were going to call me tomorrow. But some insensitive prick had taken it to social media before the rest of the immediate family had a chance to process what happened, let alone be informed.

I was angry no one called me sooner.

What a fucking predicament to find out during a baby shower. How does a parent break the news to their children? How would my eight-month pregnant sister take it?

Losing my Uncle Glenn is one of the toughest losses I will ever have to endure. This death has rocked my entire family, our hearts are in a billion pieces.

He was my rock, my number one, my saving grace. Growing up, he was the only sober adult I could count on, and he never let me down. He was my favorite lunch date: roast beef French dip at Hofbrau on the Embarcadero with a side of clam chowder, or taquitos and carrot cake at Taco Temple in Morro Bay. And he'd always take me out for ice cream. Whenever I was sick, he would bring me sugar-free popsicles to soothe my fever. He spoiled me rotten.

I'll never forget the time I watched him pick up some punk (beating his girlfriend) by the shoulder (with only one hand) and launched him off the front porch. He dragged him across the driveway and shoved him in the car and told that woman-beater to get the fuck out of our town.

I was safe and protected as long as my uncle was around. I could *always* count on him. The first one there to bail you out of whatever the fuck you got yourself into. He could fix anything, anytime, and anywhere. And now he was gone.

Uncle Glenn was supposed to walk me down the aisle.

He was supposed to be the one to take my kids on their first motorcycle ride for the love, appreciation, and thrill. I'm grateful to have been brought up by a bunch of grizzly-looking gangsters, but no one compares to him.

My brother nailed it on the head when he said, "There is something to be said about leaving this world doing what you love," and that is exactly what my uncle did.

Dear Thomas,

My eight-year-old niece Alice does her virtual school learning at my house a few days a week. I was helping with her homework in the living room when someone wearing a hoodie let themselves into our home. It took a moment to process, then I followed him down the hallway. I slowed as I turned the corner to make sure he didn't have a gun.

"Excuse me!"

He turned around, looked at me.

"I live here," he said.

"No, you don't!"

"Oh. Okay."

He didn't argue and casually walked to the door. I kindly opened the door and followed him out. He had parked in the driveway and kicked off his slippers like he lived here.

I ran into the downstairs house and yelled at all three female tenants to keep the doors locked, then took down his license plate and called the cops.

Is this what the fuck our world is turning into? Is this what happens in Lāhainā now? Homeless people just walk into people's homes in the middle of the day, hoping no one is there so they can squeeze in a nap? What the fuck?

Officers arrived and took photos of where this intruder came from and where he was headed—one of the bedrooms to obviously take a nap.

"That was fucking weird," I kept telling the officers.

After they left, I sat Alice down and we talked about how it could have gone a lot worse. He could have attacked *all* of us. I explained to her that if he had attacked me, I would have needed her to grab my cellphone, run, and call

911. And I explained to her that if she couldn't find my cellphone, then to just get the fuck out of the house and scream for help. It put things in perspective that we need to discuss emergency plans more often.

About thirty minutes later, my roommate yelled for me.

"The homeless guy is back!"

He had pulled into the driveway again. This time all the house doors were locked. I called 911 to get the cops back here but he left before they arrived.

They circled the neighborhood looking for him.

I have no idea where his car went, but there he was again, walking to the house, and just as he stepped into the driveway, the police arrived.

"Get on the ground!" one of the officers yelled.

All the neighbors were standing outside wondering what was happening. He was handcuffed, patted down, and placed in the backseat of the police car.

The neighbor two houses over rushed over to let me know he used to live in this house. He apparently grew up here and clearly wasn't taking his medication.

What year does this guy think it is?

I felt better knowing this was an isolated situation and not a random homeless person walking into a stranger's home to sleep, shower, or rob the place, but *fuck!*

"The state will automatically charge him with trespassing, unauthorized entry, and something more severe because there was a minor in the house," one of the officers said. "Do you want to press additional charges?"

"It's not necessary. I just want him to get proper help."

November 5, 2020

Dear Thomas,

I loved waking up to you this morning, and I loved you bringing me breakfast in bed. I have been waiting for that moment since my 24th birthday, and now you have done that five years later. I am beyond blessed with the love I am showered with each and every day from friends and family, and now you. My phone has been buzzing nonstop.

While you were at work yesterday, you insisted I walk around the mall and pick out a birthday present. I stumbled into Michael Kors and picked out a beautiful purse and matching wallet. Thank you for making me feel special. I have such a beautiful life.

The icing on this birthday cake happened at 2:41 this morning. We were wide awake, texting back and forth with my mom while my sister was in labor. Eighteen minutes after my birth time, Harlyn made his grand entrance into the world. It's wild. My mom became a mother on November 5th, and twenty-nine years later became a grandmother on the same day. I cannot believe I got a nephew for my birthday! I wish I could carry him around inside my new purse.

Thanks to this little dude, I will never be alone on my birthday.

December 25, 2020

Dear Thomas,

We woke up wearing the matching Christmas pajamas you picked out for us. Before a Zoom call with our families, you and I exchanged gifts. You went all out and hooked me up with a mani-pedi certificate to use on Maui, and a full set of dive gear—custom fins, pink snorkel mask, and a dive bag to carry all my new gear. Freediving is something you and I get to do together now. I gave you Rick and Morty shirts with a matching tumbler; silly things, but you love them. My favorite gift I gave you was a silver chain necklace, something you used to wear but pawned off years ago. I wanted to get you one last year but you weren't allowed to wear jewelry inside Sand Island.

We went out for a delicious sushi dinner and took a photo next to the giant decorated tree on Kalākaua Avenue. This has been a perfect Christmas and I am grateful I get to spend a few more days with you.

I cannot wait until next year when we will be in Kona. Your mom will be smiling with a full heart when she looks down on us from heaven as we spend Christmas with your dad for the next years to follow.

You have three more weeks until you're officially done with Sand Island's rehab program and no longer on probation. I am counting down the days, Thomas. I am ready for you to come home. I am ready to start our own air conditioning business. I am ready for us to finally have our life together. The life I never gave up on. The life I put all my faith, love, and energy into. I love you so much, Thomas. Merry Christmas and Happy New Year!

February 25, 2021

Dear Thomas,

The past two years, I was expecting you to come home sometime around January 17th, which marked two years of rehab, but now it's close to the end of February.

We were playing a waiting game for paperwork to go through your probation officer to confirm you were allowed to leave Oʻahu. We waited for a confirmation from Young Brothers to ship your work van from Honolulu to Kahului. You got the go-ahead three weeks ago and as soon as the van was scheduled to ship, I started the official countdown. I stapled together a paper chain-link, something I did in kindergarten counting down to the last day of school. I hung this on my bedroom door and cut a link every day. It was satisfying to watch the paper chain shorten.

Yesterday, I spent the entire morning cleaning the house and making sure your side of the closet was ready for you. I got to the airport twenty minutes early, manifesting that you land early. I have waited so long for this day that it didn't feel real. I started jumping up and down as soon as you stepped off the plane.

"You're home, you're home, you're home!"

"I know, finally!"

I kissed your gorgeous face and skipped to the car. You were ready to get to your new home, our home. Taya decorated the entryway in blue and green streamers with a Rick and Morty themed "Welcome Home" sign. Kaed cooked our favorite sesame-crusted ahi steak. It was a perfect first night home together.

We slept in this morning and the first thing you said was, "It's so quiet here."

It still hasn't hit us that you're home. You spent the last three years in jail, rehab, and living in a crowded city. We had waited patiently for this moment.

March 11, 2021

Dear Thomas,

Many years were taken away from us because of the choices you made. I never gave up on you, and we finally get to have our life together.

I wanted to spend the first few weeks catching up on lost time and being together, making memories at the beach and going on hikes and relaxing. We have spent time in the water together, but we also have a business we need to start before the hot "busy season" of summer. We need to get our name out there and let people know we are available.

Back in October, I secured a website domain. Then Tom helped buy the work van and you registered the LLC under the company name I came up with. I put everything together a month before your homecoming, created the business email address, bought an iPhone, and chose a fun, easy, catchy phone number for customers to remember. I designed the logo and ordered uniforms and business cards with a space for future customer referral codes. I setup profiles for Instagram, Facebook, Nextdoor, Google, Yelp, and LinkedIn, and hired a CPA. I downloaded a field service scheduling program, along with QuickBooks.

"What are you up to?" you asked one day.

"I have been working on your business all day."

"It's *our* business," you said, and it warmed my heart knowing you want to build a life with me. "Are you sure you're up for being the secretary?"

"The *secretary?* Wrong title. Besides being the co-owner, I will be managing this company. We've been talking about this dream of yours for awhile and I am making sure it comes to light."

Once you moved home, all that was left was to open the bank account, meet the HVAC suppliers, and purchase a million-dollar general liability insurance policy.

We live on an island, so news spreads fast with coconut wireless, yet how were we supposed to convince people they need our services?

I didn't grow up with air conditioning, so I certainly didn't know the systems needed to be cleaned on a regular basis, and I'm confident thousands across Maui don't know how—or even realize they need—to clean their AC. We need footage of you cleaning mini split systems; people need to see the horrific before and after photos. So, I sent out a mass message to our closest friends and family, letting them know we are excited to open our company, and offered a complimentary cleaning. All we asked for in return was to spread the word.

We started getting calls and texts from our friends, filling up our schedule. It's good practice using the field service software, which automatically sends texts for appointment confirmations, reminders, and invoices.

Today was our first appointment. I enjoyed being in the field with you and learning the HVAC language. We ended our first workday eating at Subway and paid for our lunch with the company card. It tasted better knowing it was a business expense.

We already have two appointments scheduled tomorrow. This promotion is working, and I'm happy to be getting footage so we can market our services on social media.

Thomas, we did it. We are officially in business!

Dear Thomas,

These past few weeks, I have scheduled two appointments per day. It's surreal. The promotion worked wonders. We started a legit business! Yet I was worried there weren't appointments on the upcoming week's schedule. I couldn't help but be nervous, wondering, *Are we going to get enough business to survive?* And then in a single day the phone rang enough times to fill the following week's schedule.

"How did you hear about us?" I asked.

"I googled 'air conditioning Lahaina' and your company popped up."

We are having fun and I appreciate learning the industry. My roommates overhear me speaking this new language, using words like condenser, compressor, air handler, fan coil, capacitor, mini split, clogged drain line, broken blower wheel, ECM motor, and condensation pump. I am quickly learning QuickBooks and bookkeeping. I even woke myself up the other night talking in my sleep with "accounts receivable / accounts payable."

The guy you worked for on Oʻahu has clients on Maui. He called and ordered you to service his client's air conditioning units.

"Shut that shit down," I told you. "You don't work for him, and he needs to respect that we have our own company now. He never calls to see if we could service *his* clients."

He refuses to introduce himself to me, or thank me, considering I'm the one who filled his 'help wanted' ad with you on Oʻahu, but I guess some men completely dismiss women as badass organizers and company managers.

Every morning you start the day with an AA meeting.

At first, I was too tired to wake up early. I'd still be sleeping, and you'd kiss my forehead before leaving for your meeting. Eventually, I started joining you to show my support. It was uncomfortable in the beginning, until I started getting to know everyone.

I decided to make your favorite cookies to share with everyone in celebration of you being sober for 1,000 days. I spent four hours baking 150 cookies last night. It would have been cool if I made 1,000 but they would have been extra small.

The meetings start off with recognizing those celebrating milestones: being sober for twenty-four hours, thirty days, ninety days, or one year.

"You're celebrating 1,000 days. Are you going to share?"

"No."

"Why the fuck not?"

"We don't celebrate 1,000 days."

"Why the fuck not? It's a milestone. One *thousand* milestones. It's a big fucking deal to me and your dad. It should be for you, too. You should celebrate *every* milestone."

Everyone cheered when you shared the news, because it is important.

And everyone loved my cookies.

Dear Thomas,

I have waited six months to meet my nephew. My mom, sister, and nephew flew to Maui on Mother's Day. This was the first time you met any of my family. I made lunch reservations at Mama's Fish House. Harlyn loved you! He wanted only you to hold him. I look forward to having our own baby one day. We've talked about it, and you want one sooner than later because you don't want to be an "old" dad. I don't think it matters how old you are, especially since I am six years younger than you and I'd be carrying the child. I would like to get our business established and pile money away a few more years before we start a family.

For the first time, I left the business phone with you while I took my family to Hāna. You didn't want to take responsibility for it, but I made it easy for you. I had pre-typed paragraphs so you could quickly text customers our availability. Lucky for you, no one called, so you had a relaxing day off.

We were at the beach when my sister brought up that it was time to have a service for our Uncle Glenn. It's been eight months since he passed, and we hadn't had a celebration of life because of the pandemic. We just started this booming business, and it's a pain in the ass to get back into Hawai'i with swab tests and quarantine restrictions.

"Thomas needs to come too," she said.

"No way. I am not introducing him to family at a *funeral*."

"It's time for him to meet the family and see where you grew up. It doesn't have to be about the funeral."

"Well, we could visit his sister in San Francisco. She just had a baby."

So, later that day I asked you, "Would you want to take a trip to California? We'd visit your sister and then I could show you my hometown?"

"Yeah, that would be awesome."

We went to our favorite sushi restaurant for my mom and sister's last night on Maui. After dinner, we all walked into a jewelry store to see if the engagement ring you and I had looked at a couple months back was still there. It was. I tried it on in front of everyone. I think about that beautiful diamond ring every night and hope no one buys it before you do.

May 23, 2021

Dear Thomas,

We were walking at sunset like we do each night when I saw the pink roses at the end of the beach. You got down on one knee, opened the white box, and revealed that perfect diamond ring I had been dreaming about for months.

"Will you marry me?"

"Fuck yes."

You were so nervous. I helped you put the ring on my finger and started crying. After everything we've been through, after everything we've overcome, we survived your darkest days. I never gave up on you. Everything I fought to not give up on was for this very moment. Dreams do come true and I fucking love you and I am so lucky to have found my person.

I had a feeling our roommates were around. As soon as you secured the ring on my finger, I looked up and they were there capturing everything on video. The tourists renting the beachfront Airbnb were cheering for us. The neighborhood kids ran up yelling, "Congratulations!" and when we started walking back home we bumped into a friend on the beach. I showed him the ring.

"That looks like an *engagement* ring."

"It is. I said, 'fuck yes.'"

"When did this happen?"

"Just now."

He looked at you and smiled, then said, "She earned it."

Yes, I did.

Dear Thomas,

I texted all my closest friends and family that we were engaged, but as for the rest of the world, I wanted to keep this special moment to ourselves before blasting it on social media.

Bryan from Colorado flew in a couple days later and I hadn't told him yet. He was in his Uber on the way to our house when I decided to post our announcement. As soon as he got out of the car, his first words were, "Do you have something you need to tell me?"

I showed him my ring and he congratulated me. He knew this was something that would make me the happiest woman in the world. And then you met him for the first time. It was cool Bryan was in town when we were celebrating your mom's birthday and your 36th. I even picked up a German chocolate cake since that was your mom's favorite.

Everyone sang Happy Birthday to Barbara, and for you.

As I was cutting the cake, Bryan asked you, "When did you know you were going to marry my best friend?"

"I was in a bathtub," you said. "I was super fucked up. She was washing my staph infection when I 'came to.' I looked up at her and knew I had to marry this woman."

Dear Thomas,

When my sister was visiting, I bought our plane tickets to fly to California this July for my Uncle's service. She submitted a permit application to host a party and reserve the barbeque and horseshoe pits at our favorite park. She even applied for a liquor license because it was required, and hired a band to play Grateful Dead songs. My estranged dad, my godfather, my uncles, and their friends decided to ignore all this.

I found out last week they planned their own service for *today*.

They knew my sister was planning a celebration of life for the end of July, but apparently that weekend wasn't going to be good for *them*. Not one of those assholes thought to call to invite me, let alone give me adequate notice.

My sister gave everyone plenty of time to take off work. There were many people traveling from out of town (me the farthest). When she found out, she made a point not to go. She felt like the barbeque at the park *they* were putting together was mediocre and not how his life should be celebrated. She felt undermined and disrespected.

I am beyond hurt. I am also not surprised.

One of my Aunts decided not to go, showing support for me and my sister, knowing how hurt we were. We were all devastated by his death. We were close to him, and for no one to invite us to his funeral was a fucking slap in the face.

I have been sad all day today.

When you got home, I was leaving to get a massage.

"Are you mad at me for something?" you said.

"No. It's the day of my uncle's funeral."

You didn't remember, although you knew I had been upset for days.

Later, when I got home from my massage, I expected you to comfort me, to hold me, but you didn't. I cried in the bathroom while you watched cartoons.

"Do you even care that I'm hurting?"

"Of course, I care."

"You're okay watching cartoons with me crying in the bathroom … feeling betrayed by my family?"

"Come lay down and watch cartoons with me."

"Thomas!"

"I know you are hurt, but I don't think any of your uncles are out to get you. I don't think they meant to hurt you by not calling and inviting you to the funeral."

"They didn't think at *all*. How could they *not* think of me? This has been the hardest loss for me, and they know it. Are they upset because they don't make the top three deaths I'll ever have to bear? My top three are my Uncle Glenn, Gabriella, and *you*."

Dear Thomas,

We were at an AA meeting when we bumped into your friend, Lacey. She's not my favorite person. She's been a bitch to me in the past. I also keep my guard up around her because I know she's best friends with your ex who broke your heart so badly in the past.

She, along with your other friends, had given up on you long ago. She didn't send you a birthday card while you were in jail. She didn't give a shit about you.

"Thank you for never giving up on my friend," she said to me.

"Mm-hmm."

"*I* did. Me and Jojo were like, '*fuck* Thomas.'"

I didn't appreciate her thanking me. I went through hell and sure as shit did not do it for her or for your friends. I did it for the love you and I share for each other.

"Well," I said, "since we are all three here together, *sober*, let me be crystal clear: I won't be saving his life like that ever again."

She looked at me and then at you with her eyebrows raised and said, "Don't ever fucking relapse again, Thomas."

"Trust me," you said. "I'm done with that shit."

Different people come and go into the rooms of AA. This morning I recognized one of your friends, a flight attendant. She and I are Facebook friends, but we've never met.

The two of you were hugging it out when the meeting ended. She loves you like a little brother. I was looking forward to officially meeting her, with my engagement ring on my finger, but the two of you ignored me completely.

When she left, I asked, "Why didn't you introduce me?"

"I thought you knew each other."

"Not in person. It would have been nice to meet her and remind her that her little brother is still alive, because of my love for you. Instead, I stood there like an idiot."

"I'm sorry."

This isn't the first time you have ignored my existence and avoided introducing me to your friends. I don't know what it is you're embarrassed about, but it's fucking rude.

July 22, 2021

Dear Thomas,

I had the strangest dream last night. We were in the grocery store and I was looking at seafood while you were standing off to the side. You were on the phone with your ex-girlfriend, Whitney, and you kept calling her "baby." This went on the entire time I was trying to pick out what to cook for dinner, and then I got frustrated you weren't helping. "Why are you calling her that?" I snapped. "Hang up and help me!" But you just kept talking to her, calling her "baby."

Super fucking random.

I questioned whether or not I should share this dream with you. Whitney has been a sensitive subject in the past, but that chapter of your life ended a long time ago. It's been well over five years since you last had contact with her. We don't keep secrets from one another. We tell each other everything. So, I decided to share my dream.

"It was so weird," I said.

"Yeah, that is weird."

Dear Thomas,

Four months in and business is booming.

We were stoked to buy a second utility van. The car salesperson asked who had better credit. You pointed at me.

"What the fuck does that matter?" I said. "We're paying with cash."

We were at the Minit Stop gas station in Lāhainā filling up the van when you started laughing and said, "Remember when you use to buy me cigarettes on your lunch break here? And now we own a business together."

"We've come a long way," I said, and smiled.

You ask all the time, "Are we making money?"

"I'm sure we are."

"How do you not know how much we are making?"

"There is a lot to bookkeeping you don't understand."

I mentioned this conversation to my grandpa. He laughed and said, "I never asked your grandma about the numbers. I did my job and went where she scheduled me to be. She managed the finances and paid the bills." As a kid, I spent the summers at my grandparents' house. I would watch my grandma run their pool-cleaning business from the home office while my grandpa went out and did the blue-collar work. They made the perfect team.

Just like us.

I ran a report the other day and discovered we have already brought in over $100,000 in gross sales. I won't tell you how much money we spent on advertising and word of mouth promotions. We also offered a fundraiser for my friend battling breast cancer. If anyone called with her "code," we donated $100 of their invoice to her treatments.

And you spent a Sunday volunteering and giving free air conditioning services to a guy who lost his wife and is raising five kids alone. We're so busy we don't even have sex anymore. We want to, but we're fucking tired.

"We should have sex soon," I said the other day.

"Yeah, that would be nice."

We both laughed and fell asleep. We have no problem working our asses off to establish the foundation of our business. We have several vacations planned later this year: Iceland for my 30th in November, our wedding December 2nd, and then finally spending Christmas at your dad's in Kona.

Today was another busy day. Before I knew it, it was after five o'clock and I remembered it was your dad's birthday. I felt like an asshole because it was nearly the end of the day when I texted him.

"Holy fuck! Happy birthday, Tom!"

"There's my Dani girl."

I love your dad so much. He is the best dad I could ever wish for myself. I'm lucky to be a part of the family.

Dear Thomas,

Today's the original day we were supposed to have the funeral my sister had planned for my uncle. I texted your sister that we will be visiting her the end of October. Then we will drive to Morro Bay so you can meet my family. We're going to have a birthday party celebrating my 'dirty thirty' and Harlyn's 'wild one.' We will spend a week there before we fly to Iceland.

You were in bed all day watching cartoons while I cleaned the downstairs house for our new tenant to move in. Meeka texted you asking if you'd tag along to an AA meeting.

"Do you want to go too?" you asked me.

"Yeah, I'll go."

Meeka picked us up on the way. There weren't a lot of people at the meeting so everyone took their time sharing.

"I have a great life," you shared with the group. "I own my own business, there is food in the fridge, and I go to sleep next to a beautiful woman, but I am still trying to figure out who I am and what I want."

What you *want*?

Isn't this life what you want? Isn't everything we've been working for what you want? I looked at you with confusion, but also sadness that you are feeling lost.

The first thing you did when we got home was turn on Adult Swim. I tried to cuddle and be cute, but you wouldn't even pay attention to me.

"Why won't you cuddle?" I asked.

"I just don't like to cuddle."

I leaned in to lay my head on your shoulder.

"Baby, please," you said. "Just give me my space."

You looked extremely annoyed.

"What's your deal?" I said. "I'm not asking you to change the channel. I wouldn't dare interrupt your time with Rick, Morty, Peter Griffin, Cartman, Kyle, or Butters. You can't watch TV with your arms wrapped around your fiancée?"

"Baby, my heart doesn't *love* like your heart does?"

"What is that supposed to mean?"

"I'm not in love with you."

Dear Thomas,

After you confessed that you're not in love with me, there was no hug or any kind of comfort. Paralyzed and in disbelief, I couldn't catch my breath.

"Why did you ask me to marry you?"

"I thought that's what I wanted."

"How do you not want this?"

"Baby, I don't know. I need to figure some things out. I need space. I need to talk to my sponsor. I need to talk to somebody about why my heart doesn't feel love."

"Thomas, if you saw me with another guy, would that bother you?"

"I don't think you should be dating anyone else—"

"I didn't say I am going to go date someone else. I am asking would it bother you if you saw me with another guy, because I would throw up if I saw you with another girl."

"Baby, I'm not going to be dating anyone."

"Would it bother you if you saw me with someone else?"

"Yes. I think so."

"That's a sign you're in love with me. That's jealousy and rejection. It says you want to be with me, and that you're in love with me. How can you say your heart doesn't *feel* love?"

"I don't know. You tell me all the time how much you love me. It's uncomfortable."

"You're uncomfortable that I tell you I *love* you? Do I need to remind you of the hell you put me and your parents through these last few years? What you put *everyone* through? Every day we feared you were going to die from an overdose."

You didn't say anything.

"I am not going to take moments with you for granted. I will tell you 'I love you' a hundred times a day because I *can*, and I *do*. I will never piss away an opportunity to express my love for you."

Is this conversation really happening?

I couldn't stop crying.

"You're acting like we're breaking up," you said.

What the fuck? It sure feels like it.

"I want to still date you," you said. "I still want to be with you."

"Are we still getting married in December?"

"I don't know. Can we just keep doing what we've been doing, like normal?"

Normal? What the actual f—

"Do I still wear my ring?" I asked.

"If you want."

Want?

"Why did you make me start a business with you?"

"If you don't want to do this, we can shut the business down right now."

"Are you kidding me? *That's* embarrassing. We provide a service Maui needs. We'd be letting the community down, and we already have an enormous clientele."

I watch so many people run their mouths, say they're going to do something and don't follow through, or change their minds shortly after starting. I'm not an indecisive person and I know what I want, and I know what I don't. I never waste my time. We started a legit company and five months later I'm supposed to shut it down? It's pathetic.

"If you don't want to be a part of this," you said, "I understand, I'll buy you out."

"No, I started this company! I'm not going to sit here and watch my utility vans drive around town with the logo

I created. I built our reputation. I've put so much into this business, so much effort into us. We make the perfect team. The community needs *us*."

I found myself crying on the bathroom floor.

"I don't want to start over!"

After staying up all night not sleeping, those words still haunt me this morning. I couldn't get out of bed, waiting for you to tell me last night didn't happen.

What do you mean you're not in love with me? You don't know what you're talking about. This is love. Do you need an example of what love *isn't?*

I thought about it, then told you, "It's okay, you don't need to be in love with me like I am with you. I still want to marry my best friend."

"I just need some time to figure things out, maybe talk to someone."

Why wouldn't you marry me?

I love you.

You'll never meet someone who loves you more than me. You'll never meet anyone who will do more for you than I have. I never abandoned you when you relapsed, while you were in jail for ten months, and rehab for another twenty-four. I had stepped up and already committed to "till death do us part," but now you have to *talk* to someone?

It's Sunday morning, the one day of the week we sleep in. You went to Starbucks as usual and brought back iced coffee and breakfast sandwiches. We were in bed with the shades closed for a few hours. I looked and felt dead, and refused to leave the room. I didn't want our roommates to see me, to see *us*. I couldn't tell them, not yet.

Later, you suggested we get fish tacos at your favorite food truck. I didn't have an appetite, but knew I needed to eat something so we snuck out the back because I didn't want anyone to see us walking through the house. I couldn't say anything to anyone because I didn't know what the fuck was happening.

How do you expect me to fake it, like everything is *normal?*

I stayed in the van while you ordered. I stared out the window like a zombie. You handed me my food. I took two bites, then spit it out and cried into my hands.

"Baby, please stop crying. Can we please just go back to the way things were? We aren't breaking up."

If you're not in love with me, after everything we've *been* through, after everything I've *done* for you, when the fuck will you be in love with me? This obviously isn't going anywhere, so what's the point? This feels like a breakup.

When we got home, you pulled into the driveway but I couldn't get out of the van. You opened the door and stared at me. I was so sick to my stomach. I eventually stepped out, still zombie-like, and invisibly made my way to the back door to sneak inside.

"Why did you ask me to marry you if you're not in love with me?"

"I was in love with you at one point."

"When?"

"When I was living on O'ahu."

"You only love me when we're on different islands? When did you realize you were no longer in love with me?"

"Maybe a month after I moved home."

"After you moved *here*, the month we started our business? Why would you do all that if you weren't in love with me?"

"Because you're smart and we make a good team."

"So, you played along to open the business, even though you *knew* you weren't in love with me, and *still* proposed?"

"I thought if I asked you to marry me, my feelings would change, but they didn't."

"Why would you ask me to marry you?"

"I knew it would make you happy."

"This is not making me happy!"

"You did so much for me. You were the only person who didn't leave me when everyone else did. I felt like I owed you."

"You're damn right you fucking *owe* me. And after all that, you don't *love* me?"

I crawled back into bed and cried while you sat there and watched cartoons, refusing to comfort me, incapable of love.

August 2, 2021

Dear Thomas,

It's day two of 'I don't know what the fuck is happening with us.'

I went on a seven-mile hike with a close friend because getting outside is the safest thing I can do for myself right now. She saw my diamond ring, examined it.

"Congratulations!"

"Thank you," I said with a fake smile, which hurt.

"When are you getting married?"

"Exactly four months from today. December 2nd."

I was in a trance most of the hike, keeping this dark secret to myself.

Am I getting married in four months?

I'm not confident I am. My friends don't deserve to be deceived, and I don't deserve this deception, confusion, and pain.

Dear Thomas,

I have been chipping away at my debt the past thirty-two months, and this morning I made my final payment. I have worked so hard for this. I expected to celebrate with a dinner or a potluck with friends. I expected to scream at the top of my lungs "I'm debt-free!" But I am distracted by my feelings of heartache. Debt-free is not hitting me. Maybe it will next month, when I don't have a payment to make.

I hope I can inspire someone else to stop spending money recklessly, to cut up their credit cards and start working toward a debt-free life.

Almost three years ago, there was a day my credit cards declined four times at three different locations. How the fuck was that even possible? I worked too fucking hard not to be able to put gas in my car. I was also two weeks behind on paying rent at the time. I had pulled into a random parking lot to cry and felt absolutely defeated. Six credit cards. Two bank loans. A car loan. The normal shit. To the ignorant, a wallet full of plastic comes off as "successful," when in reality it's an avalanche of debt.

My hairstylist introduced me to Dave Ramsey's baby steps and his book *Total Money Makeover.* I went gazelle-intense working seventy hours a week. Full-time concierge by day, Lyft driver by night. I squeezed in babysitting hours, marketed wellness products, sold random crap online, and rented my car on Turo. I sacrificed time with friends and became obsessed with budgeting, penny-pinching, using three squares of toilet paper, cutting kitchen sponges in half, cutting open toothpaste tubes, eating quinoa, beans and rice, and more rice and beans.

In the first twelve months, I paid off $19,965.42. Cue the pandemic and I paid off $7,614.87 while piling $8,000 into savings, because there was no telling which direction 2020 was going. In the first eight months of 2021, I paid off the final balance: $11,284.99. By following Dave Ramsey's advice, I paid off $38,865.28 in thirty-two months.

All by my fucking self.

Now the plan is to save $38,865.28 in the next thirty-two months. I fucking did it. I am debt-free before thirty!

I shared this success on social media and hundreds of people left comments:

"Congratulations, this is amazing."

"So freaking proud of you."

"Well done, this is impressive."

"Way to go, fucking awesome."

"Good for you."

"You're such a badass."

"You rock."

"You are the shit, bravo."

"Love seeing posts like this about growth."

"This is hotter than any boob or ass picture."

"You give us all hope."

"We all need to hear this."

"What an incredible story!"

Those who were inspired reached out, saying, "You're an inspiration, teach me," or "I'm following in your footsteps and purchasing the book," or "I already have the book but reading this post makes me want to get serious," or "You gave me goosebumps reading this."

My closest friends have witnessed this journey of mine the past thirty-two months. One time Gabriella sent me money on Venmo because she hated the thought that I was only eating rice and beans. I was no joke broke at the time.

Friends and family chimed in with things like, "You have an amazing work ethic and have great clarity to get your priorities in place," or "You worked so hard, look where you are now!" or "Never doubted that if anyone could do this, you could," or "You inspire me daily, what an experience!" or "Love how proud you are of this amazing achievement!"

This has not been a quick or easy journey.

It could have gone on longer, but it could have been *much* shorter. I can't help but think of all the money I had spent on flights, hotels, Airbnb, and rental cars for every trip I made to Oʻahu to visit you. All the cigarettes, nicotine gum, fast food, candy, and beer. Not to mention the $10,000 cash I fronted to start the HVAC company. And now you're telling me you're not in love with me? After all that? I could have annihilated my debt so much sooner. I know I spent thousands on interest, but how much of that interest was because of *you?*

You haven't even muttered the words "congratulations" today. Do you have any idea how big of a deal this is for me? Apparently not. And isn't it ironic *you* were the one who helped me get my first credit card six years ago?

I needed to share this success with my family, friends, and online followers. Everyone's kind words have contributed to celebrating, but what's crazy is that not one person knows what I am going through in my personal life. Not one person is aware that you blindsided me four nights ago. Everyone's kind words have been amazing, exciting, and supportive, yet I can't help but feel confused, heartbroken, and numb.

I am supposed to feel on top of the world today.

You took that away from me.

Dear Thomas,

I have never been so fake in my life. The past two weeks I have been faking it in front of my roommates, my friends, and I am avoiding social media.

I won't be able to handle everyone pointing and laughing at me, saying "I told you so" after the hell you put me through: your drug relapse, making myself available for those routine phone calls from jail, and holding everything down while you lived at Sand Island for two years. I cannot face this humiliation and I don't want anyone to know.

I want sex, but you won't touch me, you won't kiss me, you won't even hug me.

"You said you wanted to still *date* me?" I said.

"I don't think we should be in this relationship anymore. I should move out."

"Where the fuck are you going to go? You can't afford your own place on Maui."

"I'll find somewhere to crash."

I had my life planned out with you. Our future included getting married, going to Iceland for my birthday, and visiting your sister and my family in California.

We discussed still going through with our trip to San Francisco and going to my hometown for my birthday, and then going to Disneyland. You have never been to Disneyland and always wanted to go. Your parents always promised you and your brother that you'd go, but your mom drank away all the funds. It's becoming clear as day that you don't want to go to California with me. I'm thinking I should go for my birthday and then stay awhile. I need to be with family. I need Gabriella. I need Harlyn. I need to go home.

"Don't rush moving into the wrong place and jeopardizing your sobriety. Why don't you stay here with my cat and take care of the property so I can go home for a few months."

"No," you said.

"That's the *least* you could do for me. Let me go home."

"This is your space, and I want my own space."

"I get that, but you're supposed to take care of the maintenance around the property. That was the deal with you moving in here. You can't afford to live anywhere else."

"I don't want to stay here."

Last Saturday night, I was making dinner when you left your phone on the counter. We never go through each other's phones. We never have the desire or feel the need to. We have never had trust issues (unless you were hiding in the bathroom shooting heroin into your arm). I found myself staring at the phone I bought you for your birthday three months back, and felt the need to go through it because this entire break up doesn't make sense.

I went through your text messages: nothing. Facebook messages: nothing. Instagram messages: nothing. And then I heard you coming from around the corner.

"What are you doing?" you said.

"I posted something on the business Instagram. I wanted to see what it looked like from your profile. Let's look at it together."

You watched me go to the search bar in your Instagram to look for our company profile, but there was only one profile in your recent searches. Whitney.

What the fuck?

"Why are you searching for your ex-girlfriend on Instagram?"

"I wanted to see what she was up to."

"Why?"

"Babe, she lives 3,000 miles away."

"Why are you interested in what she's doing?"

"I was curious."

"Have you talked to her?"

"Yes."

"When?"

"A couple weeks ago."

"You called her a couple weeks ago? Where?"

"What do you mean?"

"Where were you when you called her? Where was *I?*"

"I don't know," you said, and took the phone.

"Yes, you do. Were you in the backyard? Were you in our bed? Where were you when you called her?"

"I was probably driving or working."

"How did you get her number?"

"I asked a friend on the big island for it."

"Why did you call her?"

"I needed to make amends."

"Why wouldn't you tell me that?"

"I didn't want you to get upset like you are now."

"I'm upset because you kept this from me. I have been the most supportive person in your life when it comes to your recovery. Why wouldn't you tell me, 'Hey babe, I need to call this person because I need to make amends'? I would have supported that. I don't appreciate you going behind my back. It's fucking shady." I grabbed your phone.

"What are you doing?"

"I'm searching for her contact."

"Give me my phone back."

"Delete her number. *Now.*"

I watched you delete her number, then after more arguing I watched you unfollow her on social media.

"Have you told your dad?"

"No."

"Call him right now. Call your dad and break his fucking heart."

The next night I met up with my girlfriends for a sunset hike and picnic to celebrate three birthdays in the group. I still wore my engagement ring, pretending everything was fine because I still hadn't told a soul you were leaving me.

And tonight I met with Meeka and her friends to celebrate *her* birthday. I sat there with a fake smile. They asked how our business was doing and I let them know it was doing well—the only honest answer of the night.

Dear Thomas,

"Have you talked to anyone?" you asked.

"No. This is humiliating."

"Danyelle, you have to talk to your friends."

"I don't want to talk bad about you to anyone. I don't want to put a bad taste in anyone's mouth about you."

That was my logic, in case we worked it out.

Our breakup reached another level when I took my ring off. It's a huge step in moving forward, whether I want to or not. Continuing to wear my engagement ring is not going to make you change your mind about me.

My friend Nicole is in town for a couple weeks. I met up with her for lunch on Saturday. She saw me, smiled, and immediately exclaimed, "Congratulat—"

"Don't."

"What?"

"There's nothing to congratulate me about."

"What is going on?"

"He's leaving me."

"What?" she said, as blindsided as I was. "First of all, I *can* congratulate you. You started a business, *and* you paid off almost $39,000 of debt. That is amazing. Let's talk about that, and then we will talk about the asshole."

She's right.

We talked about how I took out a mountain of debt, the success of the business, and my upcoming runaway trip to the mainland.

Nicole opened up about her fiancé, who left her two weeks before their wedding. I had no idea she was engaged, let alone had paid for a destination wedding in Bora Bora.

She understood the pain I was going through. She had isolated herself in a motel room for two weeks, hiding from the world, not wanting to speak or hear from anyone.

This is exactly what I have done the past two weeks. I never knew I could relate so close to one of my friends on this subject. This must be why I needed her to be the first to know.

After lunch, I drove to Kīhei because my close friend Holly was in town for an eighteen-hour layover. I met her at her hotel room.

"I have to tell you something," I told her.

She was ready and paying attention intently, and then she pointed at my left hand. I could tell she wondered where my diamond ring was.

"Yeah, that's what I have to tell you." I started crying and explained that you were not in love with me.

"Did he relapse?"

"No. He is not in love with me. That's it."

"And he asked you to marry him?"

"Yeah. He thought that if he put a ring on my finger it would make his feelings for me stronger, but that is not how it works."

Holly shook her head in shock.

"What about the business?"

"We are going to make it work."

"It's unfortunate he proposed in the first place, if he wasn't sure of his feelings. I have to respect him for trying to do the right thing by letting you go."

"Maybe we are better as friends and not life partners."

As I was expressing to her how much my heart hurt, and my fears for the unknown future, you called and interrupted our conversation with your inability to take care of yourself.

"When are you coming home?" you said. "I'm hungry."

"There is plenty of food to cook in the house."

"Could you pick something up on your way home?"

"No, there is food at home."

It's interesting how comfortable you are asking me to buy, bring, or cook you food … after you shattered my heart.

Yesterday, I went hiking with Meeka. I was fighting to bring myself to tell her, the words wanting to burst out.

"I can't do this!" I said, sobbing.

"Dani, what the fuck is going on?"

"He's leaving me."

"What?"

"Thomas, he's leaving me."

"Are you fucking kidding me?"

"No, he told me he is not in love with me. He's moving out today."

"Oh my god!"

Her heart broke for me. She knew better than anyone what I went through over the years, *for* you. She knew how deeply I had always been in love with you. She knew how happy I was with you, under the impression that you loved me back. She knew you were the luckiest man alive to have an angel like me.

We continued our hike while Meeka went through all the emotions I had been going through over the past two weeks—shock, confusion, sadness, denial, anger.

The stages of grief continued at the nail salon.

It's been a week since you told your dad. He has not sent me a single text message to check on me. Not even the three words 'Are you okay?' If your mom was alive, she'd be calling ten times a day to make sure I'm okay, which I am not. So, I proceeded to remove every family member or close friend of yours from my social media accounts. Fuck anyone who associates with you. You embarrassed me. I don't want your family or friends to know anything about me.

You were washing the van when I got home. I walked right up to you and said, "You make me *sick*. You have humiliated me to the point that I don't want anyone to know anything about my life. I fucking *hate* you!"

You had nothing to say. You eventually came in to pack your bag with clothes, but the rest of your crap remained in my closet.

"Don't forget the rest of your shit."

"I'm not taking this stuff right now."

"Why not?"

"I am crashing at a friend's until I find a place to rent. I'll move it then."

"So, I'm your storage facility?"

"I have nowhere else to store it."

Who the fuck do you think you are? How could you do this to me?

You have left for good, and now that you're gone I have to face my roommates, because at some point they will notice you're not here.

I called Auntie Anne first, and was crying when she answered.

"What is going on? Who do I need to hurt?"

I caught my breath and said, "Thomas left me."

"Oh my god."

"I wanted to let you know that he won't be living here anymore."

"What happened?"

"He's not in love with me."

"Fucking asshole."

"He just moved out, so I needed to tell you first."

"You haven't told Taya?"

"No, I'm going to tell her when she gets home."

"I am so sorry. I am so mad! He just had to fuck everything up. You are going to get through this. I love you."

"I love you too."

Taya and Kaed are in the middle of opening their own private luxury picnic business. Before I texted her, she texted me.

"Are you and Thomas free this Tuesday at five o'clock?"

"We're not :("

"Shucks. Do you two have a free night any time this week? I want you to schedule me in your calendar for a fully loaded picnic."

A private romantic picnic in the park; that would be sweet. Only if you were in love with me.

I didn't respond for two hours.

"When will you be home?" I texted her later.

"Five minutes."

"I need to talk to you. Will you come to my room when you get home?"

I heard the front door open, then footsteps down the hall. She came in the room smiling and hopped on the bed.

"Hey! What's up?"

"Um …" I took a deep breath and shrugged. "There's no other way to say it, so I'm just going to say it. Thomas left me."

"What! What happened?"

"It was two weeks ago. He told me he is not in love with me. I've been avoiding you this entire time."

"I knew the energy was different, but I assumed you were stressed about the business."

"I didn't know what to say because I didn't know what was happening, and now he has officially moved out."

"I don't understand."

"I was fucking blindsided."

"You didn't see this coming at all?"

"One hundred percent fucking blindsided."

I asked Taya to break the news to Kaed because the words coming out of my mouth were unbearable. Telling three people today was more than I could handle. I also told her to tell Piper the next time she saw her at work. I couldn't face her. I couldn't get myself to say the words, not even in a text message. Piper has seen me cry rivers over you in the past. She would never want to say 'I told you so.' She would never want you to give her a reason to say those words.

Taya invited me for a sunset walk, but I wanted to keep hiding in my bedroom. I got up in the middle of the night for a glass of water. I walked down the hallway and felt a sadness that you no longer live here. It's not our house anymore, just mine. I waited a long time for you to move home so we could finally spend our life together, and after five months you're gone.

I have no idea how I fell asleep last night but I did. I woke up exhausted to the sound of you stomping up the staircase outside my room at 6:30 in the morning. You were on your way to your AA meeting but wanted to make sure I was 'okay.'

When you turned around to leave, I asked for a hug.

It baffles me that I have to ask you to hug me. You say you care about me, but you don't think to hug me? You don't *want* to hug me. What is your definition of caring?

Today is also the ten-year anniversary of Gabriella's mom passing away. It's also the four-year anniversary of when you and I called 911 in Kona for the ambulance to take your mom to the emergency room, when she officially started dying from alcoholism.

I texted Gabriella to call me. I needed to confess why

I had been hiding like a hermit, avoiding social media, and ignoring text messages. The more friends I share this heartbreaking news with, the more real it becomes. I have lost the love of my life: *you*.

The phone rang and it was Gabriella.

"Hello?"

"Hi Danyelle-ee. What's going on?"

I started crying.

"Why are you crying?"

"Thomas left me."

"What? Did he relapse?"

"No."

Are you noticing a pattern? She listened to me cry and expressed her shock. *I* never saw this coming; *she* never saw this coming; *no one* saw this coming, except you.

"What are you doing with the business?"

"We are still going to be in business together."

"Are you sure that's what you want to do?"

"We make a good team, which is why this is so sad. We make the perfect team. We have brought in over $150,000 in five months."

"You need a lawyer and a contract."

"No, that's not necessary. He wouldn't do anything to screw me out of the business. He knows he can't run the business without me."

Dear Thomas,

I broke the news to my other roommates, one by one. They deserved an explanation why they only see you in the driveway loading equipment.

"Dani," Mia said, "I made an extra plate of pasta for Thomas."

"He won't be coming home tonight."

"Oh?"

"He doesn't live here anymore. Three weeks ago, he told me he's not in love with me."

"Wow," she said slowly. "I had no idea. You know how to keep it together, sister."

"I spent a lot of time in my room avoiding everyone."

"I noticed. I could feel tension between you two, but thought it was work related. I did *not* see this coming."

"Neither did I."

Anthony hasn't noticed whether you're here or not, I know that. He's an older dude living his best life, but he saw me at the table fighting back tears while washing dishes.

"You okay, D?"

I shook my head no. "I haven't had the chance to tell you because it sucks to say it out loud, but Thomas left me. He doesn't live here anymore."

"Are you kidding me?" he said softly and stared down the kitchen drain.

These are my roommates, my friends.

And I wanted to throw up when I told my walking buddy Kristine.

"If Thomas changed his mind," she said, "and decided he *did* want to be with you, would you take him back?"

"As heartbroken as I am, my answer has to be no. If I took him back, it would always be in the back of my mind whether he's in love with me or not, or when he's going to change his mind. I'd have to go through this pain all over again."

I have been avoiding talking to Bryan in Colorado. It's too humiliating. He was always skeptical about why I never gave up on you. He thought I was crazy. Just like Piper, he has the same opportunity to say the words 'I told you so,' but I know he won't because he never wanted this to happen to me. I couldn't call him, so I called his friend Douglas instead and told him to pass on the news. He didn't exactly pass it on; he told Bryan to call me ASAP.

Bryan FaceTime'd me. "Danyelle, what's up?"

I couldn't bring myself to say it. I only cried.

"You don't have to say anything." After a long pause he said, "So, what … he relapsed again?"

"No, he didn't relapse. He was never in love with me."

"I don't believe that."

"Believe it."

"I'm so sorry."

And then I hiked with Izzy this morning. She knows you and I sleep in on Sundays and enjoy Starbucks in bed. She told me not to rush picking her up, but I told her I would love to start our hike early. She didn't know my easy Sunday mornings ended weeks ago.

"What's new?" she asked a minute into our hike.

"Thomas left me."

"What do you mean?"

"Three weeks ago, he told me he's not in love with me. He moved out last week."

"Three *weeks* ago?"

"Remember the sunset picnic hike a few weeks ago? I

was faking it the entire night. I was still wearing my engagement ring because I didn't know what was happening."

"Oh my god, Danyelle, I knew something wasn't right that night. You didn't have your usual spark and pep in your step. That's why we met early today, isn't it?"

"That's exactly why."

"Dammit, Danyelle. I am so sorry. I have been asking Meeka and Taya for two years now whether or not he's a good guy for you. When I saw the video of him proposing, the look on his face was similar to my ex-husband's. He was not in love with you when he proposed. I could *feel* it. That's not the way you deserve to be loved. I'm sorry you're hurting, but I have to thank Thomas for letting you go. You deserve to be loved."

September 9, 2021

Dear Thomas,

It's been a rough month, but I woke up feeling positive yesterday and decided I was going to have a good day. I didn't want to bury myself in bookkeeping and scheduling. I needed to do something creative for my soul. We've been in business for six months but don't have a website. Websites are "old school" because everyone uses social media, but I have been asked many times, "Do you have a website?"

I paid for a domain almost a year ago. I created the tabs, picked the color schemes, added our business hours, phone number, and email. The only thing left was to upload our logo. I did not have the vector files saved onto my computer and couldn't find them in our company email, so I opened another Gmail tab to search through my personal emails.

"What the fuck is all this?"

On the top-right corner were your initials: "TW."

Holy shit, you hadn't logged out of your Gmail!

In the middle of your inbox was a United Airlines flight confirmation for you and Whitney.

Whitney? What is this shit?

You had booked plane tickets to fly into LAX on November 7th to spend a week with her in Malibu, but your departing flight is out of San Francisco on November 14th. This means at some point you will be near my hometown, while I am there.

You fucking asshole.

Once we decided we wouldn't be going on our vacation together, I said I needed to go home and be surrounded by family. You asked if you could still have a week off in November, and I declined because we'd be losing an unnecessary amount of business. You told me you wanted to go to the big island to visit your dad and go diving with your buddies. I reminded you that you have two weeks in December to spend with them around Christmas. You pushed that you deserve a break, and now I realize you wanted time off to visit Whitney.

I called Meeka, freaking out.

"I am going to beat the shit out of him later."

"Don't do anything that would put you in jail."

"There aren't going to be any witnesses."

So much for wanting to feel positive. My creativity shifted from building our website to breaking your bones.

I wanted to call and scream at you, but you're in the middle of the workday, and your work affects my pay and my reputation. I spent the rest of the afternoon pacing in the living room, the hallway, and staring at myself in the bathroom mirror.

Eventually, I calmed down from the initial shock and anger of discovering those emails, so I texted you to come over after work so we could talk.

"This has been extremely painful. If there is anything you're going to be doing in the future that would upset me, I would rather hear about it directly from you than find out from someone else, or on social media, or any other way. Do you understand?"

"Yeah."

"Is there anything you need to share with me?"

You paused, assessed, and shook your head.

"No."

"That's fucking bullshit, Thomas!"

"I'm not hiding anything from you."

"You think I am that stupid? I found your fucking *plane tickets!* You're flying to California to see Whitney the week of my birthday! The same week you were supposed to go to California with me!"

"How did you find my plane tickets?"

"I find out everything, and just gave you the chance to be honest with me."

"It's none of your business," you said, and the tone in your voice was disturbing. You never spoke to me like that.

"Fuck you!"

I slid off the bed and grabbed a shoe from the floor. I swung it at your face, left to right, then right to left, *hard*, and when you put your hands up to protect your nose, I came up from under your chin and then slammed the shoe down on top of your head. I threw the shoe and started slapping and punching you. You turned to walk out the door, but I shoved you into the bathroom door, face first.

My roommates heard the commotion and ran into my room. When they realized I was beating the shit out of you, not the other way around, they shut the door and allowed me to continue without interruption.

"Stop!" you finally said.

I took a step back to glare at you while you were trapped in the corner, your face as red as a Kula Farms strawberry.

"I am not going to come over here after a long day of work to be assaulted and be told I am a piece of shit!"

"You *are* a piece of shit!"

"No, I'm not!" you said, finally showing emotion. "Danyelle, I was going to tell you about my trip to California, but I was going to wait until you healed some more."

"Oh really. What, in just two more months I was going to be *cured* of heartache?"

"No, I don't think that. I thought the initial pain would have settled by now. I'm surprised you're still hurting. I had no idea you were in love with me *this* much."

Seriously?

"Who the fuck do you think you are? You don't get to decide when it's a good time to tell me something you know I don't want to hear. You don't get to decide what I *can* or *cannot* handle. I gave you the opportunity to share something before I found out another way, and you blatantly lied to my face. You can't grasp the concept of slapping me with the truth. Instead, you would rather kiss me with lies. You didn't honor the ninth step in your program: 'make direct amends to such people wherever possible, *except* when to do so would injure them or others.' You did injure me when you went behind my back and called Whitney to supposedly make amends. You destroyed our relationship."

"I'm sorry, Danyelle. I should have never moved in with you. I should have been single for a year when I got back to Maui, like my program suggests."

"What the fuck are you talking about? So, it was okay to be in a relationship while you were in jail and rehab, but not okay when you moved home and started a business? How about you be single for an entire year after dumping your fiancée *before* you pursue a relationship with Whitney?"

"No way. I am not heartbroken like you are. I have patiently waited for her for a very long time."

"You're a piece of shit and I fucking hate you!"

After you left, I called Tom and told him I had just finished rearranging his son's face with a size-ten Nike shoe.

"He deserved it," he said and laughed.

"He lied and said he was going to Kona to visit you in November."

"Wow. I didn't know he pulled me into his lie. He told me he was going to California, and I told him he better tell you before you found out on your own. And I was right."

"You knew he was going to California?"

"He's flying into Los Angeles and then he and Whitney are going to drive up to San Francisco to visit his sister."

"Are you kidding me? That's the vacation I planned for us. He would never come up with the idea of visiting his sister on his own. That was me."

Your dad and I ended our conversation when he told me you were calling him on the other line. I waited forty-five minutes before I called you.

"How are you feeling?" I asked.

"Not great. I'm upset, and shocked. I've never seen this side of you before."

"Where and why the fuck would you have seen this side of me before? You've never given me a reason to beat the shit out of you before. You've never betrayed me before."

"It didn't need to resort to violence."

"Don't act for a second like you didn't deserve that."

"That was unpleasant."

"You deserved it, and you know it. Why the fuck are you going to California the same week I'm going to be there? The same week you were supposed to be there with *me*?"

"I want to see if I have feelings for this girl. I don't know … maybe I'm only in love with the idea of her. I'm going to California to explore these feelings."

"The week of *my birthday*. The same week and same place I had planned for *us*. I wanted to take you to my hometown, Thomas. You fucking broke my heart. This trip you are taking is beyond inappropriate. You have zero fucking respect for my feelings."

I couldn't get out of bed this morning. Every bone in my body hurt, caused by the adrenaline of beating the shit out of you. I can't recall the last time I hit somebody that hard. But I'm also smiling because I canceled your plane ticket, and I am the only one who knows.

September 13, 2021

Dear Thomas,

I am bothered you're going to California to spend time with Whitney so soon after our breakup. What's the rush? You're just friends, and she made it clear a long time ago that she is not in love with you.

You are in the field today and I can't focus because the controlling need to be one step ahead—the investigative side of me—has my head spinning.

I logged into your Instagram and went through your messages, but there was nothing interesting. Whitney's profile wasn't interesting either. Then a private message from her came through: a video. I started a screen-recording before opening and all I saw were nipples.

What the fuck is going on?

Friends do not send friends steamy naked videos from the bathtub.

Does she not know about our relationship, the one you just destroyed? I don't believe you ever told her we were engaged. I have to give her the benefit of the doubt, but this needs to get cleared up *now*.

I got her phone number from her art website. I called, but it went to voicemail. I called again, and after a couple rings she answered.

"Hello?"

"Whitney, this is Danyelle."

"How did you get my number?"

"It's posted on your website. Are you open to talking to me? Thomas won't tell me anything. Maybe you can help me out."

"I feel a little ambushed here."

"Come on, Whitney, answer my questions, woman to woman."

"Okay."

"Thomas told me he had to call you to make amends. Is that true?"

"Yes, he did owe me amends."

"Did you know we were engaged?"

"Yes."

And you're already sending naked videos?

"You knew we were engaged. Did you know this little trip to California he planned to see you was the vacation he and I were supposed to be on?"

"You're going on vacation to California together?"

"We were, until he decided to go behind my back and call you. Now you're having a vacation together, the one *I* planned. How does that make you feel?"

"Danyelle, what's going on between him and me is none of your business."

"How can you say that, you insensitive bitch?"

Whitney started crying and said, "I'm a really compassionate person."

In what world?

"No, you're a fucking cunt. Thomas and I were engaged. We had a wedding date set. What the fuck are you doing?"

"I'm sorry, but I can't help the way I feel. I have loved him since I was a kid. He is my soulmate. If he asked me to marry him tomorrow, I would say yes."

Wait, what? She's in love with you? You are her soulmate?

"Then where the fuck have you been this entire time? You knew he wanted to be with you, so why haven't you been together all these years?"

"It just didn't *feel* right. I'm an intuitive person. When I saw him last, I had a bad feeling something wasn't right and he ended up relapsing later that year. People were calling and telling me I needed to come to Maui because Thomas needed me, and I asked them to not tell me what was going on. I didn't want to know about him being at his worst."

"He probably relapsed because you broke his heart and *abandoned* him. I know you left him before. You didn't stick around when he was using. You never helped him."

"I stayed as long as I could, but I couldn't watch my best friend kill himself. My skin felt like it was on fire all the time. I was suicidal."

"Please, you're preaching to the choir. Do you have any idea what he and I have been through the past six years? You left him a long time ago. I didn't!"

"I didn't even know he was still alive."

"Did you ask anyone for an invitation to his funeral?"

"Last I heard he was in jail."

"Yes, for *ten months*. You never asked *one* of your Maui friends where you could send him a love letter for ten months? They all knew where he was because I let them know. Did you send him any condolences when his mom died?"

"That's not fair."

"You're telling *me* what's not fair? Do you have any idea what we've been through? And now you're telling me he's your *soulmate?* That you'd marry him tomorrow if he asked? You have obviously never been to a wedding. 'I take you in *sickness* and in health.' Have you ever heard those vows? No, you can't handle him. You refused to handle him at his worst, so why the fuck would you deserve him at his best?"

"I don't know what you want me to say, Danyelle. He called to make amends and I asked if we could have another conversation. I'm starting to regret I asked him to call me."

"The right thing would have been to not interfere with our relationship and take part in *ending* our engagement."

"We have always had this connection I can't explain," she said. "He gave me a promise ring a long time ago and we never actually broke up."

"Don't even fucking go there. You *left* him, and you have lived with several boyfriends over the past ten years. And a *promise* ring? I had the *engagement* ring. I paid my fucking dues. He is alive because of me."

"Thank you for doing what you did to save him."

"I didn't do that for you. In fact, had I known everything I did was for him to leave me so you two could have your life together, I would have left him to die in the streets of Waikīkī. Just like all his friends did. Just like *you* did."

The conversation went silent.

"Can I ask you some questions?" she said.

What the fuck could you possibly ask me?

"Do you believe he is your person?"

"I know he is my person. If he wasn't, I wouldn't have stuck it out this long."

"You said you were together for six years?"

"Yes."

"Have you heard of me before all this?"

"Yes. You were a problem at the beginning of our relationship. He was afraid to commit to me because of how badly you had hurt him. The only word he ever used to describe you was 'bitch.' His mom told me all the time she couldn't stand you. And you know what sucked the most? I was there when his mom was dying. She was on all sorts of medication and in some of our final conversations she was confused and kept calling me 'Whit.' It hurt, but I didn't let it bother me. She never liked you. All she knew is that you hurt her son. She told me all the time what a fucking bitch you were, and she wished Thomas would get the fuck over you."

"Okay. Do you share a phone plan?"

"Yes, we share a fucking phone plan. Everything he has is because of me. He is incompetent without me, and he likes me doing everything for him."

"So, do you see our text messages?"

"No, I am not able to read your conversations," I said, with the naked video of her in the bathtub burning in my head, "but you and Thomas going behind my back having private conversations while we were engaged, and while he was living in my house, feels like cheating, and you're a fucking homewrecker."

"Your feelings are completely valid. I know it hurts, but trust me, this is the best thing that will happen to you. This is for the better."

"You're just saying that so you can have your 'soulmate' to yourself."

"No, I'm not, Danyelle. Him letting you go is the best thing to happen to you."

"You don't get to say that shit to me. Those are words my best friends get to deliver. Not you."

October 13, 2021

Dear Thomas,

How the fuck do you live with yourself?

I have always been cursed with a stress cough. Ever since I discovered the real reason you broke up with me was to be with Whitney, my cough has escalated to throwing up. Today I was driving in the pouring rain, crying hysterically, thinking about how you broke me, destroyed me, how you stole my light. And so, I called you.

"Why did you do this to me? I did not fucking deserve this!"

I screamed those words so hard I threw up all over myself in the car. A new low. I looked like the fucking heroin addict. I didn't even recognize my own voice.

I felt broken, like the most fragile ornament ever thrown off a second story balcony into the middle of the street, then shattered into a million pieces, and then a massive truck running over those pieces and turning them into a billion smaller pieces.

That's how broken I am. All because of you.

You did this.

It's been almost ten weeks since you told your dad you were leaving me. During that time, I have spoken to him twice. Both times, I reached out. Not once has he reached out to me. Not once has he sent a three-word message like "I am sorry" or "Are you okay?" It fucking hurts. Tom and I were close, and I was lucky to have him as a father figure.

I feel more than replaced; I feel abandoned.

And I haven't heard from your brother or his wife either, and I don't expect to hear from your sister since she's home with a newborn. If your mom were alive, she'd be calling me every day. She would be disgusted by what you've done. She loved me, and adored me, and she always told you, "Don't you dare fuck it up with Dani." God, I miss her.

It was time for me to send a text message to both your dad and brother:

"I am extremely hurt that not one person from this family has reached out to me to ask if I am okay. I am far from it. Is this what it feels like to be replaced? I called Whitney and she had the balls to tell me that if Thomas asked her to marry him tomorrow she would. And then she had the audacity to thank me for everything I have done for Thomas. Keeping him alive. Not abandoning him. If I had known everything I did was for Thomas to eventually leave me for that fucking bitch, I would have left him in the streets of Waikīkī to die. Thomas never wanted any of this to happen, or so he says. I could have healed from the humiliation of him breaking my heart, but his actions have been evil, conniving, malicious, unforgivable, and heartless. He is spending my birthday vacation in California with Whitney. And he has already planned his Christmas in Kona with Whitney. To say I am extremely hurt is an understatement. Thomas has absolutely ruined me, and I fucking hate him. I wish him zero happiness. I was deceived and made to be a fool. I wish someone from this family would have told me to kick rocks a long time ago because apparently there was already a Mrs. Walker in mind. I guess Whitney has been 'the one' all along and I am replaceable which blows my mind because if Thomas ever got into an accident causing him to be a quadriplegic, that bitch would never leave her life in Malibu to wipe his ass for the rest of his life. I proved I would, as his wife, but now he won't be my problem anymore. This is the last time the Walker family will ever hear from me. Consider me dead."

Dear Thomas,

I have been counting down the days to get the fuck out of here, and today is the day. I have been hiding in my house for two months, not wanting to see or be seen by anyone. The only time I go outside is to run in the dark.

"Aren't you afraid you'll get attacked while you're out running alone?" people ask, but I am so fucking angry right now that I dare someone to come at me.

Let's see what would happen.

I avoided talking to my mom for the month of August. I called my sister first to tell her that you and I broke up. I had my sister tell my brothers and extended family. It took me six weeks to finally tell my mom. She cried, knowing how happy I was with you. I told her everything, but I left out the part about you being with another woman. I haven't told anyone about Whitney. The only people who know about her are my roommates.

I went to dinner with my cousin the other day. I told her how I felt used, and how you deceived me. She said I dodged a bullet, and she's not the first person to tell me that.

Everyone has mentioned in some form or other, "It's a good thing you *didn't* get married," but I am embarrassed we didn't get married. At least I would have accomplished something. It would have made all this count. I am most angry that you asked me to marry you in the first place. Divorce is normal. So what if our marriage didn't last. The fact that our engagement didn't make it to the alter is humiliating. You should have never proposed.

Now what? I heal, fall in love, someone proposes to me, and I am supposed to say yes in hopes they won't leave me two months later? You ruined that for me.

The past two nights, I unexpectedly broke out in hives. I have never had hives before and didn't know what the fuck was happening. I was itchy on my thighs and the back of my arms, and within hours it spread over my entire body. I thought I had Chickenpox. I don't keep medication in my house, but thankfully the hives were gone when I woke up the next morning. But it happened all over again last night, and at the same time!

What the fuck have you done to me, Thomas?

A few weeks ago, you asked when I was leaving for my trip to the mainland.

"Why do you want me off this island so bad?"

"I want you to heal," was your answer.

"You just want me to heal so you won't feel guilty for what you've done."

"Yeah, that's a part of it."

"Fuck you."

For the first time ever, I am getting on a plane to run *away* from you, not to run to your rescue, and it's an unfamiliar feeling.

Dear Thomas,

I have been staying with my friend Xavier in North Carolina the past two weeks because I want to be as far away from you as possible. A place where I only knew *one* person.

We went to the State Fair, and I sent you photos of the giant stuffed Pickle Rick pillows because you love *Rick and Morty*. Then I texted a photo of me enjoying a churro with fireworks in the background. We were talking on the phone that night about the business when I asked myself out loud, "Why the fuck am I sending you photos of my trip?"

"I don't know," you said, "but I like it. It makes me feel like we're friends."

"We are *not* friends. We will *never* be friends. You pissed away any chance of us being friends. You don't deserve to know anything about my life, especially anything good."

I never texted you another photo of my trip.

Xavier's sister, Sunny, has an in-your-face-no-bullshit-I-don't-sugarcoat-it kind of personality, which is the type of energy I appreciate. She is an extremely talented tarot card reader, and had no clue what I had been going through. So, I asked her for a reading.

With sage burning in the corner, she removed crystals from the tops of her decks and started flipping cards—*The Hermit* (hiding and isolating in my house), the *Two of Pentacles* in reverse (juggling something), the *King of Wands* (someone coming at me with passion), and the *Queen of Swords* (me, guarded). The *Eight of Wands* came out of every deck, which means a message is coming to me, usually an immediate message; this made Sunny raise her eyebrows and ask, "Is there something that *you* need to say?"

I looked at Xavier and wanted to throw up.

"There has been another woman the entire time."

"I knew you weren't telling me something," Xavier said. "I could sense you were holding something back."

I let it all out, crying of embarrassment.

And as I was purging everything that had happened, Sunny kept flipping cards that represented you: a wolf in sheep's clothing, a lost soul (twice), and when she pulled the devil and tower card, she yelled, "It's done! It's over!"

I told them how hurt I was about Whitney. I wanted to give her the benefit of the doubt, that she might be a good person, but Sunny validated my gut feeling when she got in my face and said, "Honey, she don't give a *fuck* about you!"

Sunny pulled more cards confirming that you are playing mind games with me, and that you are an awful karmic cycle I haven't been able to escape.

"He's waiting for you to come back," she said. "He doesn't want to lose you as a business partner."

"How am I supposed to continue being in business with him after everything he's done to hurt me? How am I going to make this work?"

"You don't need to figure that out now. You don't need to decide this second. You have a lot to process."

She pulled interesting cards about my future as well: abundancy, opportunity, something about a house, a business venture, and a large amount of money. I have no idea how any of that could possibly come about, but I will try my best to pay attention.

My reading with Sunny was intense, eye-opening, and a huge step in breaking down my walls. Yet I'm still violently throwing up several times a week. It's amazing the damage you have done. Who knew the body physically purges betrayal and deceit?

It's my last night in North Carolina before flying home, and I'm dreading your own trip to California. Xavier and I stayed up until five in the morning talking through shit. I brought up the dream I had back in July, the one in the grocery store with you on the phone with Whitney, calling her 'baby' in front of me. Am I unknowingly psychic?

Curious, I called.

"Remember when I had that dream about you talking to Whitney on the phone when we were grocery shopping? When was that, in correlation to when you called her?"

"You told me about the dream the next morning."

"So, you called her, and I had the dream the same night?"

"I guess so, yeah."

"How did that make you feel?"

"Horrible."

"Why?"

"I felt like I was cheating."

"You *were*."

The conversation got heated since you're always trying to defend and convince yourself that "emotional cheating" is not a real thing. And you didn't like it when I suggested that I meet you in Malibu. You threatened to get a restraining order if I interfered with your relationship, and I couldn't stop laughing.

"Let me get this straight … you want me to run your business, because you're incapable of doing so, but you're going to get a restraining order against me? Did *I* cheat? Did *I* betray you? Did *I* shatter *your* world? Have I caused you any pain?"

"Every day. Every day you tell me I'm a piece of shit."

"Because you *are* a piece of shit. Stay the fuck away from my hometown, Thomas, especially since I'll be there."

"I can't promise you that. I don't know where we're

going to be. I'm not familiar with California. How am I supposed to know if I'm near your hometown or not?"

How is it that I even have to ask? You *should be* telling me and *insisting* you won't go near Morro Bay. Put yourself in my position.

Imagine giving your entire life to someone and making them your world. Imagine never giving up on them, when odds are always against you. Imagine twiddling your thumbs while they're in a coma for twenty-three days. Imagine sleepless nights hoping they won't die. Imagine making yourself available every night for a phone call from the love of your life—the only fifteen minutes in twenty-four hours you ever look forward to. Imagine waiting, and waiting, and being forever patient, spending money on visits, flights, car rentals, hotels, and being faithful because you are madly in love! Imagine your dream coming true when they ask you to marry them. And then imagine them *cheating* on you. Imagine them changing plans for a vacation with their first real love and replacing you with someone who gives them butterflies instead because you're *not enough*. Imagine that …

I couldn't sleep at night if I did that to someone, but I would do everything in my power to make sure I didn't upset them anymore. Control the controllables. I would without a doubt fight to make sure I stayed far away from their hometown. I would announce it loud and clear and make it a point to not drive through their town, especially while I am with the person I cheated on them with. If I could control that, and spare them any more pain, I *would*.

It's sickening that you'll fight me on this. It's sickening that you make yourself sound like you agree, but then have to wait for me to cry to honor my simple and reasonable request. This entire betrayal is sickening.

You fucked me over, Thomas.

You used me.

You cheated on me.

You continue to hurt me.

You're going to do whatever the fuck you want to do, regardless of how I feel. Zero fucks given.

"Just fucking keep her away from me and my life," I texted you, "stay far away from my hometown. Grow the fuck up and take control of the GPS while you're in California. After all, this is *your* vacation, right?"

"Danyelle, I do respect all your wishes and will abide by them. I am sorry about what I've done. I don't know how to get you to know that. You're gonna start feeling better soon. Trust me, it's right around the corner. You're gonna be okay. I know you don't think so, but you will. I still love and care for you. Call me a liar all you want. I want you to be happy."

November 5, 2021

Dear Thomas,

I flew to California days ago and have been hiding at Gabriella's house, not ready to see anyone. I was crying last night because it was the last night of being in my twenties. I had my entire life planned with you, which you derailed.

Today I am thirty, single, heartbroken, and the idea of having children is nowhere in sight. I had been planning to spend my thirtieth witnessing the northern lights in Iceland with you, but you had other plans.

I have done a lot in my first thirty years of life. I auditioned for *American Idol*, swam with dolphins, stood under waterfalls, cliff-jumped, and zip-lined enough times to never do it again. I have played with elephants in Thailand, and had front row seats witnessing a friend give birth. And my biggest accomplishments, besides graduating high school at sixteen, was losing over forty pounds and paying off almost forty thousand dollars of consumer debt.

Things have happened to me that I pray will be one-time occurrences, like being evacuated from a fire in the middle of the night, unknowingly spending a family afternoon with an organized crime boss, and visiting you in jail. I have not lived a boring life.

I am currently living a *painful* life. I genuinely have no idea what to expect or what to look forward to in my future, but that shouldn't take away the fact that I have so many experiences for which to be grateful. I have so many memories that make me smile.

Tomorrow, I will be celebrating my nephew's 1st birthday as I am celebrating my 30th; I will be surrounded by sixty people who love me. You are not one of them.

I spent the morning at the spa getting a birthday massage and facial. Afterward, I picked up Holly from the airport. I am so grateful she flew in to spend my birthday with me.

If there is one day of the year I refuse to work, it is my birthday, and you know that. It's the one day of the year that is all about me. I told you I would be screening business calls, especially since you have created the habit of calling me after every job to review what needs to go on the invoice, and to tell me when to send it. It is 2021, Thomas. All service techs run off of apps on their phones. And you are more than capable of editing and sending invoices. You are just fucking lazy and want me to do everything for you.

It amazes me how many times a day you call just to hear my voice. You're the co-owner of this company. Why don't you take responsibility for billing your customers? You want to get paid for your services? Send the fucking invoices. You don't call me at the end of the workday; you call me after *every single* tedious job. You knew I would be taking today off and celebrating over the weekend, but instead you told every customer I would send their invoices the following Monday. Are you fucking kidding me? Pure laziness.

I reminded you how easy it is for you to send an invoice through the app on your phone, and you threw it back in my face. You said I shouldn't have a problem doing it because it's easy for me to do. You're a fucking asshole. It's my birthday, the one day of the year I shouldn't have to do anything for anyone, especially you!

Dear Thomas,

Today was the day of the party for me and my nephew, with sixty family members and close friends. I haven't seen some of these people since before I moved to Maui nine years ago. Some drove over two hours to attend the party. Some knew about my broken heart, some didn't and were probably expecting to meet you, and some had no idea I was engaged.

I had prepared myself to not take photos and to just live in the moment, surrounded by loved ones. Because we invited so many people, I tried my best to catch up and pay attention to every guest. I was definitely going with the flow and not paying attention to what time we cut the cake and beat the piñata. My sister did a great job staying in charge, even though today was her day too—her son's first birthday.

She put together a "this or that" game to see who knew me best. Before the party, I had to choose my preferences between living in a house or in an apartment, if I'd rather be four feet tall or eight feet tall, a famous musician or actress, a hero or villain, born in the past or in the future, smart or pretty, have an afterlife or cease to exist, have money or fame, freedom or security, if I'd rather give or receive, have love or success, and last but not least, be cheated on or be the cheater. That was the fucked up question and it took me the longest to decide.

I have always been cheated on, but I have never cheated. Since being cheated on sucks, would I prefer to be the one doing the cheating? No, I am not a horrible person. I don't use people or waste their time. I am not you.

Dear Thomas,

Today is the day you are planning to fly to California, even though I canceled your flight back in September. I woke up to a text from you.

"You have any idea how much money you owe me now? Every time you cancel my flight it costs more to rebook. Trust me, you do not want to go down this road!"

Technically, I only canceled your flight once.

"What are you talking about? I canceled our flight when you told me we weren't going to San Francisco together."

"I'm talking about my flight today!"

"I didn't cancel your plane ticket, Thomas."

"Well, it's canceled!"

"It's not my fault you don't know how to book a flight. What airline did you use? Airlines are understaffed. Maybe they canceled your flight. Did you think of that?"

"No, I didn't think of that. Sorry."

"Don't ever threaten me with bullshit like 'Trust me, you do not want to go down this road.' Learn to do shit on your own. Take some responsibility."

"I'm sorry, I said that out of anger. It was wrong."

"Where was that threat six years ago? It would've been nice not to have gone down the road of falling in love with you, committing to years of jail and rehab, and building your dream company. It would've been nice not to have gone down the road of humiliation after you cheated on your fiancée with some stupid bitch you never got over."

"I'm sorry."

"Do you need me to call Whitney to let her know how you like your dick sucked? Maybe if she doesn't do a good job, she can owe you the money for your plane ticket."

"Jesus, why do you have to get so nasty?"

"Don't ever forget what the fuck you've done to me. Fuck you, fuck your vacation, and fuck Whitney."

That conversation set the tone for the rest of the day. Thank god Holly is still in town. We drove to a beach in Morro Bay and spent a couple hours with my sister's family. I was too angry to pay attention to anyone, and instead stared at the ocean thinking about you boarding your plane to fly here. I hadn't told anyone about you coming to California, and it's true that secrets make you sick.

Holly and I were sitting at an outside table having a vegan lunch at Shine Café when I said, "I have to tell you something. There's more to my breakup story."

She put her fork down, and asked, "What's her name?"

I told her how you went behind my back to call Whitney, that you wanted to make sure she was single, available, and on board with you leaving me. And then I told her you were currently on a plane to California to spend this next week with her.

In five minutes, Holly found Whitney's Malibu address. We debated driving there. It would have been one hell of a savage road trip, but we decided to let karma run its course.

We decided to go axe-throwing instead, and it turns out I'm pretty good.

I suggested to the owner, "You should sell photo prints so I could throw an axe at my ex's face."

"Throwing a weapon at someone's photo is considered a threat."

"A threat, or therapy?"

Dear Thomas,

We are missing a lot of business this week because you decided to take your trip to California, not to mention your Christmas vacation next month. You genuinely think I'm on vacation, but I'm not. I'm still working. The business carries on and the phone doesn't stop ringing just because I'm not on the islands; it's a mobile phone, idiot. Work continues as normal wherever I am.

You recently "trained" another technician to work for us: Tommy. You reminded me the other day that both our vehicles are sitting there unused, and that he could service appointments on his own, *if* I had jobs to schedule for him. How convenient. Yes, that's how it works.

Tommy went out on his own yesterday and as he pulled up to the site, the older work van took a shit. Fluids and smoke shot out in every direction. I told him to focus on the job and that I'd deal with calling a tow truck. I also chased down our insurance agent because we had another customer claiming we destroyed her mattress when her AC leaked onto it. So, no, I am not "on vacation." Tommy finished cleaning the AC window unit and lost a screw, so he pulled an extra-long one from his toolbox. That screw was apparently long enough to puncture the compressor, causing the entire AC unit to explode in his face.

Not only are we not getting paid for that service, but now we have to buy this customer a brand new AC unit. We needed to replace it immediately, but Tommy already had one hell of a day between the van and him breaking the AC unit. I went into instant problem-solving mode as far as the customer's property goes. I called Lowe's and Home

Depot to make sure they had AC window units available, cross-referenced the dimensions and specifications of the power source, and then I called another one of our employees to make sure he was available to assist Tommy today with installing the new window unit.

According to Instagram, you're having a fantastic time at Six Flags while I'm juggling insurance claims, scheduling employees, ordering parts, and vomiting betrayal in the toilet.

You're not stepping up as a business owner, which is why I yelled at you to step the fuck up. The work van that broke down is registered to your name. I don't give a fuck how long it sits on the side of the road. You want it towed to a shop? *You* call the fucking tow truck.

Tommy and the other guy picked up the replacement air conditioning unit at Lowes. They installed it and disposed of the broken one. The new unit cost $600 and we provided two hours of free labor, in addition to the free failed cleaning yesterday. We are out approximately $1,000. The cherry on top was when Tommy hit a parked car with our only working utility van. He took the side mirror off someone's parked truck. He felt terrible, you were pissed, and I was absolutely loving it. I let him know he was doing me a favor.

The fact that everything is going to shit because you are on vacation with your girlfriend is making me feel better.

"Tommy is not allowed do anything else until I get back," you texted me in anger. "I don't know if I ever want him to do anything for us again. He is costing us money."

I laughed because you were the one who trained him.

"Who are you to give up on someone the first time they make a mistake? You sound like a hypocrite. It's just the side mirror. $100 to fix. It's not like he was in a head-on collision and sent people to the hospital."

On top of that, the dealership called and let me know

the van that broke down yesterday needs a lot of repairs. It's going to cost close to $13,000 in parts and labor. An entire rebuild. You said 'no fucking way' because you are small-minded.

"Let's sell the van," you said over the phone. "I'm not paying $13,000 to repair it."

"Who's going to buy a van needing $13,000 in repairs?"

"We'll get rid of it and buy a new one."

"So, you'd rather spend $60,000 on a new van instead of $13,000 on a repair, basically making it new? You *do* understand there's a serious shortage in used vehicles and they are all jacked up in pricing … I don't like the idea of spending $13,000 in repairs either, but that's our best option."

As I was explaining this logic, I could hear your GPS in the background. I didn't know where you two disgraceful love birds were going, but you were making a lot of turns:

"*Stay on Orcutt Road for … slight right onto Johnson Avenue.*"

When we finished talking business and hung up, I typed an email to the auto mechanic to let him know to move forward with the repairs. And then a painful light bulb clicked on in my head. Orcutt Road, then Johnson Avenue? You were in San Luis Obispo! Are you fucking kidding me? You were only a mile from where I was at the time. What the *actual* fuck? This couldn't be happening. You have turned me so psycho that I started googling where else there could be an Orcutt and Johnson *anywhere* else in California.

I called Holly, hysterically screaming.

"I don't want to believe it, but he's in San Luis Obispo! That fucking asshole! I asked him for *one* thing, and that was to stay away from my hometown!"

"Are you sure he is in SLO?"

"Unless there's another town in this state where Orcutt Road meets Johnson Avenue, he is in San Luis Obispo."

I called and when you finally answered I asked, "Are you in SLO?" Click.

That validated your location, you fucking sociopath.

I texted, "Are you in SLO?" No response. "If you're not in SLO, what's your issue? What's the problem with me knowing where you are? You are in SLO, aren't you?"

Is this for real? What are you doing here?

You were in Malibu and then you were planning to drive to San Francisco to see your sister. Okay, I can understand that. But why didn't you take Interstate 5? What, you wanted to take the incredibly long scenic route? What is wrong with you? I asked you one thing, *one*, and that was to not come to my hometown, especially while I was there. Fuck you.

What about the conversation we had when I was in North Carolina? You had texted me these exact words:

"Danyelle, I do respect all your wishes and will abide by them. I am sorry about what I've done. I don't know how to get you to know that. You're gonna start feeling better soon. Trust me, it's right around the corner. You're gonna be okay. I know you don't think so, but you will. I still love and care for you. Call me a liar all you want. I want you to be happy."

Every time your lips move, you lie.

You're so fucking cruel. You are a liar and a traitor. I am not friends with liars or traitors, nor will I associate with them, therefore I am not going to be in business with you anymore. You ruined our chances of building this business into an empire. You are nothing without me, and you know it. You continue to rely on me and it's pathetic. You couldn't even send one fucking invoice so I could have my birthday off. The one fucking day of the year I shouldn't have to lift a finger and yet I still had to for you because you're too fucking incompetent.

I AM FUCKING DONE!

The next thread of text messages I sent you:

"I will be forwarding all business calls to your cellphone. I am taking my name off the business account so you are liable for everything. Get a new business partner because you are fucked without me. How big of a check would you like me to write myself?"

No response.

"You don't care how big the check is?"

All I want is to drain the bank account.

"You ruined me. You absolutely destroyed my life, you coward. You turned me psycho. You destroyed who I am. I have never been so broken. You have no idea the embarrassment you have created for me, and after everything I have done for you to save your fucking life!"

Still no response.

"WHAT THE FUCK HAS THAT BITCH DONE FOR YOU? HOW MANY HOTELS HAS SHE PAID FOR? HOW MANY CARE PACKAGES? HOW MANY DAYS OF WORK HAS SHE MISSED FOR YOU? DID HER HAIR EVER FALL OUT? DID SHE EVER GAIN 40 POUNDS BECAUSE OF YOU? I DESERVED THE LIFE I BUILT FOR THE TWO OF US: MARRIAGE, KIDS, THIS COMPANY. I WORKED MY ASS OFF TO GIVE YOU EVERYTHING. I PROVED MY LOVE TO YOU AND ALL YOU DO IS DISRESPECT ME AND TREAT ME LIKE SHIT! YOU THINK I AM A FUCKING JOKE? FUCK YOU! YOU DON'T GIVE A FUCK IF I DIE TOMORROW. YOU RUINED MY LIFE."

No response.

Dear Thomas,

After your joyride through my hometown, my mom came home and found me throwing up in the toilet. I called Gabriella because she made plans for me to tag along on her family camping trip. She booked a few campsites in San Simeon. I am not much of a camper but getting out of my mom's apartment for a few days will be good for me. I have been isolating myself in California, just like I did in Maui. I broke down and started crying to Gabriella. She doesn't even know about Whitney or you driving through our hometown.

You're lucky my brothers didn't spot you.

Gabriella started crying too and said, "You need to stop with this business. It's *killing* you. You leaving this company does not mean you failed as a business owner. You didn't sign up for this! You didn't sign up to start a successful company just to have your fiancé leave you. That wasn't the agreement."

She's right. I didn't sign up for any of this.

If you would have come to me and said, "Hey baby, I could really use your help to open my dream company, and then once we establish a client base I'm gonna start fucking my ex-girlfriend, but you can still get paid by running my business from the comfort of your own home," obviously I wouldn't have agreed to that.

We camped for three nights at San Simeon. It was sunny but this island girl is always cold when the temperature outside is below seventy-eight degrees. My favorite part of the weekend was staying up late roasting marshmallows and playing campfire games. My mind was preoccupied during the daytime. Everyone was having fun playing Cornhole or throwing the football around but I couldn't help but think about how you're in California too and probably meeting up with your sister soon.

The trip I had planned for us.

I cannot believe you are taking Whitney to meet your nephew. I hope he throws up on her or cries when she holds him. I was looking forward to meeting him and your sister, because I give a shit about your family.

Gabriella and I packed up the campsite yesterday and unloaded everything in the front yard. I took a shower after not having one for four days and plopped on the couch. Then I received an interesting message from someone I know at the Henry Miller Memorial Library in Big Sur who recognized you. It's a small town. And it all makes sense now.

You and Whitney drove right through Morro Bay, and then continued up Highway 1 to explore Big Sur. Out of all the places you could have traveled to in California with her, you chose a place within miles of me. You think *island life* is small? Welcome to the central coast. Everyone knows everyone here. This is my world, and you're not invisible.

I was enjoying dinner with my nephews last night when you sent me a text that read, "Getting on a plane to Maui." Like I give a fuck.

I'm done talking to you. I do feel a minor sense of relief that this vacation of yours—which I have been dreading for months—is finally over. Go back to Maui, get back to work, and do what you do best: hurt me more.

Since I still have a business to run, I tracked your flight to make sure there were no hiccups with you getting home in time for the fourteen-hour shifts I have scheduled for you all week. The only thing remotely getting me through this is making sure you don't have any free time. You don't deserve joy in your life. What's weird is that your departure and landing time didn't add up. It turns out the plane had to do an emergency landing because birds flew into the jet turbines. *So close!* I wouldn't want anyone else on that plane to get hurt, but if you died in a plane crash all my pain would go away.

The only emotion I have felt the past three months is humiliation. I have been hiding, too embarrassed to show my face. I haven't wanted anyone to know what you've done to me, but now I am sick of people *not* knowing.

Our electrician you first met in AA—and who *I* first met in AA by going with you—always gets the business phone number mixed up with your personal number. He texted me (thinking it was you): "We seem to be missing each other lately, you wanna just throw the check in the mail?" He still hadn't received the check I told you to send him on November 3rd, almost two weeks ago.

I texted back, "Good morning! You will need to text Thomas's personal phone. He was in California this past week visiting the cunt he left me for. I believe he got back to Maui last night. Sorry I am not on island to pay you on time."

"Oh crap, okay. Didn't hear that part of it. Sorry."

"I'm sick of people not knowing what he has done to me, after everything I did for him. I'm sick of Thomas walking around high and mighty like he's rebuilt his life and on top of the world. Everything he has is because of me. He used me to open this company and then dropped me like a bag of dog shit."

"Danyelle, maybe it's for the best. True colors and all?"

"I apologize for unloading that, but I am sick of people not knowing what he has done to me. That is why I can't show my face at the AA meetings anymore. I have never been so humiliated in my entire life."

"I think you should show face. Don't back down. Be

who you are. You aren't in the wrong here, so make it known. I'll be praying for you, girl."

"Thank you."

He obviously texted you next because you sent me a message: "How much do I need to pay him for the last job?"

You're too stupid to scroll back through your messages.

"Let's be smart and mature about this," you texted next. "I know how smart you are! We need each other to help one another. And the community is grateful for us. So, let's think about the greater good instead of our personal problems."

You fucking narcissist. You just got your dick sucked all week while I was throwing up in the toilet. You want a text back after that? I'll text you back after that …

"THIS MESSAGE IS UNFAIR AND INSULTING. IT'S AN UNBEARABLE BATTLE FOR ME TO GET UP EVERY DAY AND CONTINUE WITH THIS BUSINESS. DON'T EVER TELL ME I AM IMMATURE. YOU ARE THE ONE LACKING MATURITY. HOW THE FUCK DO YOU EXPECT ME TO FEEL AND ACT AFTER WHAT YOU HAVE PUT ME THROUGH? IF WHITNEY DID TO YOU WHAT YOU DID TO ME, YOU WOULD BE DROWNING IN ALCOHOL AND STICKING NEEDLES IN EVERY VEIN. WE NEED EACH OTHER? I DON'T NEED YOU! I NEVER NEEDED YOU. BUT YOU HAVE MADE IT CLEAR YOU NEED ME MORE THAN YOU WANT ME. JUST BECAUSE THE COMMUNITY NEEDS US DOESN'T GIVE YOU THE RIGHT TO USE ME AND ABUSE ME AND HUMILIATE ME. DON'T EVER DISMISS THE PAIN YOU HAVE CAUSED. YOUR PERSONAL LIFE WILL AFFECT MY PERSONAL LIFE FOR A LONG TIME."

Dear Thomas,

Since my birthday party, I have continued to isolate myself at my mom's, crying over you. I planned on driving to Huntington Beach for a few days and then to Oceanside, and from there, backtracking to Laguna Beach, Moorpark, Oxnard, and then Santa Barbara. I don't know if I was distracted from the drive or listening to different radio stations, but for the first time, I felt okay. It took everything in me to not drive through Malibu to find Whitney and spit in her face.

I made it to Nicole's and unpacked my duffle bag since I'd be staying there for a few days. Back in August, when she was visiting Maui, Nicole was the first I ever told that you were leaving me. Now she's one of the first to know *everything*. My roommates and Holly are the only ones who know about the other woman. It's too embarrassing. It's not like you left me for some random woman down the street. No, you've been in love with Whitney our entire relationship.

I waited for Nicole to put her daughter to bed. I needed to have a lengthy conversation without interruption. It was time I let her know what the fuck has been going on. She was in shock. The only three words she could come up with were, "How dare you?" meaning you. She knows everything I have done for you and how I stuck it out and never lost hope. She could feel the weight of this betrayal. It took me three hours of crying and two boxes of Kleenex to get through that conversation.

She kept repeating, "How dare you?"

Dear Thomas,

I loved staying with Nicole in Huntington Beach. We spent the remainder of the days walking along the beach and binge-watching *Ridiculousness* for laughs. I didn't want to leave but spending a few days with Nicole was the first time I felt "okay" since my heart broke, and since I had been traveling on the mainland these past two months.

Then I moved on to Oceanside where Auntie Anne lives. I was freaking out about December 2nd approaching, the date we had set to get married. You and I figured that business would be slow and that we could take a few days off to celebrate. And if Decembers ended up being slow going forward, we wouldn't feel guilty taking annual anniversary trips.

I was right about business being slower that week. We hardly had any appointments on the books, which annoyed me. I put in extra effort to email all the property management companies that use us to let them know our schedule was light. I successfully filled it up, scheduling you fourteen-hour days. Your life is 'work all day' and 'cartoon-burnout all night.'

December 2nd came and I wasn't as depressed as I thought I would be. I opened up to Auntie Anne about everything you had done to me since the end of July. When I brought up you driving through my hometown after I had begged you not to, she agreed it was pretty fucking hurtful, and that you and Whitney will get your karma one day.

I told her how I wanted to leave the country for a few months. Leaving Maui has been nice because I don't have to see your face, but I still have to talk to you every day. It's awful. I'm trying to figure out how to hire someone to run the admin side of the business so I can disconnect for a while. But who would I hire? Who could I trust? Who would be capable?

"You need to start thinking about stepping away from the business," she said, "and don't drag any of your friends into it."

I was comfortable in Oceanside. Auntie Anne set me up with my own room. The bed was cozy and the room was dark, which let me sleep in late. I didn't want to leave but needed to start heading north again.

"Don't drive through Malibu," she said. "It's too far for me to pick you up from jail."

I made my way to Thousand Oaks next for a quick trip to visit my Oma. There was no way I was going to tell her anything about the breakup.

"Marry a man who loves you more than you love him," she told me a long time ago. It's the only advice she's ever given me, and I always wondered why I couldn't marry a man who loves me equally. If only she knew about us, it would certainly prove her logic.

I made it to Santa Barbara last night. I am staying with my uncle Jed and his wife Malia. We stayed up late talking about my dysfunctional family, my fucked up childhood, and what I want in life. I didn't get too deep into the breakup but they strongly felt I dodged a bullet.

"I am not going to be a part of the business anymore," I told them, and myself. "It's not me, it's not who I am, and it's not what I am supposed to do."

This entire time I have been fighting so hard to find a way to keep the business going, with or without you. I am so grateful I can run a company while running home and surrounding myself with family. I am fucking good at running this business, but the HVAC industry is not my passion, it's *your* passion. I was passionate about you and supporting your dreams. Now, I have no idea what the fuck I am passionate about. Until I get away from you and this business, I will never figure that out.

I am now staring at the sunset—something I haven't taken the time to do in a while—thinking about your mom. It's the four-year anniversary of her passing. What would she think of all this? What would these past four years have been like if she were alive? Would she have tried to bust you out of jail? How many times would she have visited you in rehab? How would she have handled the pandemic? Would she have remained sober? She would have been proud of you for opening your own business. She would have wanted to be there to witness you propose to me. How would she feel about you leaving me the way you did? What would she say to Whitney? How would she take it when she eventually heard me say, "All I want is for your son to relapse and die so I can spit on his grave."

December 17, 2021

Dear Thomas,

I flew to Colorado for my next stop on my journey to heal. I joined Bryan and his family on a road trip to Breckenridge, and I feel like I am in a winter wonderland, but I can't even enjoy my time here because our schedule is filling up, the business phone won't stop ringing, and now you're extending your vacation a few days early.

Saturday, December 18th through Sunday, January 3rd. You are taking sixteen days off work now, even though you're not flying to Kona until December 22nd?

Why the fuck can I not schedule jobs on the 20th and 21st then? We have been arguing about this for over a month. You told me you were flying to Kona on the 20th but your plane ticket is booked for the 22nd. When I called you out on this, you said you were going to change it to the 20th. Right, like you're going to sit on the phone with customer service to change your plane ticket two days early. Do you think I am that stupid? You can work those days.

I sent you a screenshot of your plane ticket.

"STOP READING MY EMAILS!" was your response.

"CHANGE YOUR FUCKING PASSWORD, YOU IDIOT!" was mine. "WHY IS YOUR EMAIL ACCOUNT SYNCED TO MY COMPUTER?"

You are exhausting. You are draining and disrespectful. And you are obviously hiding something. Why won't you tell me the real reason you refuse to work on the 20th and 21st? This isn't about my personal feelings. This is about you affecting our income.

I decided to say "fuck the business" for the rest of the day.

Bryan's sisters and I put on our bathing suits and ran barefoot in the snow to jump in the hot tub. It was time I told them everything. They were disgusted. It's exhausting retelling this horrible story, but I would rather they hear it directly from me.

Dear Thomas,

I spent the majority of Christmas Eve in Bryan's basement. Bryan and Douglas produced a song while I wrote the lyrics. I hadn't written a song in over ten years and once I heard the melody, the words poured out and onto the paper in less than an hour:

Baby, I'm not hearing this
Just shut up and kiss
Tell me you love me
Why you doin' this to me?
After you got on one knee
Said "will you marry me?"
This can't be happening
What about my diamond ring?
You're my everything
How did you change your mind?
Love is so hard to find
You're really gonna leave me behind?
Look at my heart bruise
After I paid my dues
All that I've been through
This can't be real
This wasn't the deal
How the fuck else do you expect me to feel?
I had my whole life planned
Marriage, kids, and career
Now everything is fuzzy
Nothing is fucking clear
You shit on all our goals and dreams

We made a perfect goddamn team
Now idk what it is you want in life
But apparently it's not *me* to be your wife
How did I fall for you?
Don't have the slightest clue
I'm so much better off without you

Writing this song, putting on the headphones, and singing into the microphone was the best therapy. I forgot how much I love making music come to life. I am finally starting to feel better, and it's because I haven't been talking to you this week.

Bryan's family is big, so everyone pulled a name for Secret Santa. I thoroughly enjoyed spending the holiday with them. Once everyone opened their gifts, Bryan's sister handed me a present. I was not expecting anything, considering I was crashing their family Christmas. I opened the small box and inside was a beautiful silver necklace with a rainbow pendant. It was a Bryan Anthony necklace, and the rainbow signified the word 'Overcome.' Inside was a beautiful message:

"The storm emerged without any warning, without any sign. She never saw it coming—a whirlwind of darkness, uprooting her present and cascading shadows over her future. A true collision of disruption and despair, she finds herself consumed by chaos, her faith unraveling as it disappears into the cries of the sky. And in the midst of heartache, she decides she can either dwell in her disasters or she can learn to weather them—she can let the storm break her or she can let it build her. It's in this moment of clarity she begins to fight her way out of darkness. It's in this moment of grace she stops running from her storm and starts following her rainbow. And despite the aches of her journey, she is led to a place only she can find—a place of courage, a place of beauty, a place of becoming. This is what it means to overcome. This is what it means to survive. And although the storm brought her destruction, it also brought her strength. She learned she is more powerful than anything that arrives to break her—the darkness will never stop her from finding her own light."

This couldn't be truer and more fitting for me and what I have endured. I was touched by this special gift. This is forever my most favorite necklace I will ever own.

December 26, 2021

Dear Thomas,

Since you are not working for sixteen days, I am making sure I don't work for the same amount of time. I setup an Out of-Office message for all business inquiries: "We are closed for the holidays and unavailable until January 3rd."

I gave up asking you to open your mystery schedule. Monday the 20th came around and the phone wouldn't stop ringing. There is one particular restaurant in Kapalua that always calls us for service, not only for their air conditioning units, but their refrigerators and freezers. Christmas is their busiest season. The executive chef called, begging for you to come in. They have over 500 reservations a night for the next two weeks and their refrigerators aren't working properly. I respect myself enough to not take the blame for this, or bullshit someone who doesn't deserve to be bullshitted.

Your actions and behavior of your personal life not only affect me, but our customers as well. Our customers deserve to know that you and I are falling apart, so if they want to have another legitimate and reliable company service them, they have a right to find one.

I let the chef at the restaurant know you are not answering my calls and refusing to work. I gave him your personal phone number and advised him to reach out directly. I assured him you were still on Maui until the afternoon of the 22nd, and that if you said you were unavailable, you were lying. He was a little thrown off but I know he called you because I got a text from you later in the day.

"I just did one hour of labor at the Kapalua restaurant. I had to defrost a coil. You can send them an invoice with one hour of labor."

Are you out of you fucking mind?

After all the arguing about your availability to work, you think I'm going to write up an invoice for you?

"So much for changing your flight, liar," I texted back. "Got several phone calls today for troubleshooting I had to turn away. You can create the invoice yourself if you want to get paid for your work."

"I'm going to block you for the remainder of my vacation. Happy holidays."

"Fuck you, and your holiday."

Before I left for the mainland in October, I had written out your paychecks and dated them for the tenth and twenty-fifth of each month. That was supposed to get you through the end of January. You had asked for an extra check for $1,000 before I left. A bonus.

"Fuck no," I said, and you argued that you work your ass off and shouldn't have to ask for money. I had to remind you that you are financially illiterate.

"We both work our asses off. We both deserve a Christmas bonus."

I agreed to that, and dated your check for December 25th. You verified it was in the pile of checks before I left. You were adamant about your extra thousand dollars. You then cashed it out, in *October!* I was furious and called you screaming.

"I took the time to organize all your paychecks ahead of time so I didn't have to mail paper checks from wherever the fuck I'd be! I already entered all the receipts in Quick-Books. It is unbelievably irritating how stupid you are!"

"A bonus is meant to be cashed out *before* Christmas," you said, "so you can buy presents in advance."

I don't know what inbred friend of yours fed you that shit but where I am from and where I have worked that is not the purpose of a bonus. Do we need to call it an "end of the year" bonus? And who are you buying Christmas presents for? What, you're a stand-up family man now?

In November, you sent me almost $2,000 of backpay in rent and bills you owed me. This means you ran out of your bonus *before Thanksgiving*, and it's safe to bet it wasn't used on Christmas gifts.

To protect the company, I turned off your business bank card for the duration of your stay in Kona; that way, you wouldn't use the company account for personal use.

Sure enough, you tried to use it, twice. I get immediate notifications on the business phone whenever the company bank card is used.

"Hope your holidays are good," you texted, "would you mind giving me the new password to the bank account?"

So much for blocking me during your holiday.

I did not respond.

December 28, 2021

Dear Thomas,

I am still staying at Bryan's house and decided last night I would be spending today cleaning his house. He is always on the road, so I wanted to help by vacuuming, dusting, and making sure his laundry is put away. He is one of my best friends and it's the least I can do for him since he opened his home to me as one of my safe havens. I was getting dressed this morning when my phone started buzzing off the counter. Notifications were flying in.

On the screen were message previews, mini-screenshots of a photo with comments like "what the fuck?" and "are you okay" and "who the fuck is this?" and "what's going on?" I unlocked my phone and opened the messages fully and wanted to throw up.

You had posted to your story a photo of you and Whitney with the words "I love you infinity." You used to use 'infinity' when describing how much you loved *me*.

So many of my family members and friends still didn't know about us until you posted that. They didn't know you had left me for another woman. They all follow you on Instagram and Facebook, so they were shocked when they opened your story and saw *her*.

I looked at it myself and discovered you not only blocked me but blocked your own company's social media accounts. *You blocked your own company.* Did you think I wasn't going to see your sappy post? Did you not want to hurt me *more?*

I ignored most of the text messages because the humiliation was overbearing. I could only talk about it with Nicole or Holly. I hadn't even told Piper about the other woman. I was physically shaking, so I channeled my anger, pain, and anxiety into cleaning the floors.

Your friend Charly in Texas called. I don't think I have talked to Charly since I scared the shit out of her over three years ago, when I called crying and she thought I was going to tell her you overdosed.

"Girl! What the *fuck* am I looking at?"

"Hi, Charly."

"I was literally just thinking about you and Thomas the other day. I was thinking about how happy I am for you two: engaged, your business booming—thinking we have to catch up—and then I see a photo of him and a girl who looks like *Whitney* with an 'I love you infinity.' What the fuck happened?"

"He left me. After everything I did for him. He let me know he was never in love with me, and he fucking called her to make sure she was single and on board with getting back together, and she was."

"I am so confused."

"Yeah, I was fucking blindsided; once when he broke up with me, and then again when that bitch told me they are soulmates and she can't help that she is in love with him. What am I missing, Charly? Last I heard, she didn't give a fuck about him."

"That's what I thought!"

"What happened all those years back?"

"I remember she got sober and he didn't, and then he did and wanted to get back together with her, but she turned him down. She was clear she had moved on and was *not* in love with him. Then she came to Maui and brought her hot new boyfriend. It was the first time I ever saw Thomas insecure. It hurt him. He'd hook up with girls, cuddle with them, and make them feel like he liked them, and then he'd ghost them because he didn't give a fuck. It was awful. He did that to *so* many women. I never understood why he couldn't get over Whitney and open himself up to love. And then I saw that change in him when *you* showed up."

"Apparently not, because he let me know he was never in love with me. He asked me to marry him because he was hoping that would make his heart love me, but obviously we know that's not how it works."

"Dude, I am so fucking sorry. I'm at a loss for words."

"Where has this girl been this entire time?"

"That's what has me stumped. Who *does* that? She is not a good a person. And you know what? He did you a favor. You are so much better than him."

"Everyone keeps saying that but it doesn't take the pain away."

"It won't go away for a long time, Danyelle. It's going to be awhile. And if I need to jump on the phone with you every week to help get you through this shit, I will help you, but you have to understand … he is broken, and he is *not* your person. If someone isn't meeting you at least halfway, they are not for you. You deserve to be treated like a fucking Queen."

I love Charly.

You have another friend, Hannah, who has always been nice to me, but she has also been deceived and is easily manipulated by you. She's too naïve to see it. She called to comfort me, but she doesn't get it. She doesn't grasp the gravity of pain you caused.

"If he had stayed with you, Danyelle, he would have relapsed."

How could she say that? I saved your fucking *life*, so many times. To say I would have been the reason for your relapse is a slap in the face.

Dear Thomas,

Last night I had dinner at my friend Dominic's. He and I worked together in college, and he was like a big brother to me. I haven't seen him in over ten years. He and his wife and two daughters live not too far from Bryan in Colorado. I gave them a heads-up I was going to need to talk to them about heavy shit, and we did. I appreciate Dominic's wife. They had experienced their own heartaches before they met each other, so they were understanding of my situation. After dinner, I realized I wasn't emotionally stable to drive. It was only a twenty-minute drive back to Bryan's but the idea of sleeping there alone wasn't comforting.

I don't know how much more pain I can take. I don't know how I can get any more broken than I already am. When I crawled into the bed Dominic had made up for me in the basement, my body wouldn't stop shaking again, and soon that turned into violent body tremors.

How do you sleep at night after causing someone this much pain?

And you did this to me *sober*.

I texted a friend who I could count on to tell me what I needed to hear.

"I am so broken. This is the lowest I've ever felt. How can someone hurt another person so bad, and be so evil, conniving, and malicious. What did I do to deserve this?"

"You're not a weak person, Danyelle," they said. "Just think about all the crazy shit you've been through and survived. You've been beaten down before, many times in life, and you always come back stronger. This is no different; it's just fresh. Ask any of your friends and they will say the same. You will get back up. You didn't do anything to deserve this. We will never understand why people do what they do."

"I just want to fall asleep and never wake up."

"Don't say that."

"I was looking in the mirror earlier today thinking how insane it is that I am surviving this right now."

"You're insane for thinking you won't survive."

I tried to focus on my breathing because the shaking was becoming more like epileptic convulsions. I turned on the TV, trying to find something light and distracting, so I put on an episode of *Down to Earth with Zac Efron* when he traveled to Costa Rica.

Recently I have been researching whether to run away to Indonesia, Thailand, or Costa Rica. I was having dinner with Bryan and Douglas at Hooters in Denver when I decided where to escape. I booked and paid for plane tickets and accommodations for six weeks. As soon as you buy me out, I will be starting the next chapter of my life in Costa Rica.

Dear Thomas,

I am back in California spending a mellow New Year's Eve with my friends. While waiting for the New York ball to drop on TV, I received an unexpected message from your cousin Ariana.

"I saw Thomas's post the other day. Are you okay?"

"Aloha, Ariana, you are the first family member to reach out to me and ask those three simple words. Thank you. And no, I am not okay. I have never been so humiliated. I gave Thomas my heart and soul. I was madly in love with him. I never abandoned him through his time in jail, or his rehab. I fucking loved him. I started this company to build our future together, and then my dream came true when he asked me to marry him. And then he told me he wasn't in love with me. He emotionally cheated on me by reconnecting with his old girlfriend, who he has apparently been in love with during our entire relationship. I could go on, but no, I am not okay. I appreciate you checking on me. Tom has not checked on me once and that has broken my heart because we were so close. I miss Barbara so much. She'd be checking on me every day."

"I am so freaking sorry. That's what I was afraid of. You were the best thing to happen to him. I miss Aunt Barb so much. She definitely would be there checking on you. If we ever get a chance to visit Hawaii, I am definitely coming to see you. I'm so sorry you're going through this. I hate that he hurt you. And I hate that he's reconnecting with a past relationship. He's going to end up back to square one."

"She will fuck him over again. I know it. They are both impulsive. They have hurt a lot of people. I would not be surprised if he kills himself when she leaves him again."

"I hate that so much. Sadly, all it takes is one person to change your life, not for the best. This is why I decided to ask you and not him."

"She has abandoned him before and has proven she won't take care of him. Barbara hated her and always loved me because she saw how much I loved her son. I proved myself. They are both delusional and their relationship is going to crash and burn. We still own the business together but it's unbearable. If he had left it at 'I'm not in love with you' I could have healed. I could have been civil and we'd still be friends. But what he has done is unforgivable. I won't be there for him the next time he falls. I gave him six years of my life and he broke me."

"I don't blame you at all. You have given him enough. He doesn't deserve any more from you."

"Ariana, I cannot tell you how much it means to me that you reached out. The entire Walker family has broken my heart. I lost an entire family. I would love to see you. Please let me know when you come to Hawaii. I am a week late, but please tell your daughter happy birthday for me. Thank you for checking on me."

"Anytime."

She is the only family member who reached out to me, and it makes sense because she is from your mom's side of the family.

Dear Thomas,

You have been calling me the past four days but I am ignoring you. You said you were going to block me over the holiday vacation, but you never stick to your word. It sounds like you're back on Maui working jobs, which is stupid because it's the weekend.

"Are you gonna answer the phone?" you texted me yesterday. "There are jobs we have to talk about."

Why would I answer the phone on a Sunday? You even left a message wishing me a happy New Year. Seriously, stop trying to be nice. You need to turn your nice-energy into not-fucking-people-over energy, or carelessly hurting those who have bent over backward for you. No one benefits from your mediocre comments or gestures.

You texted this morning at 8:50, "Ignoring calls today?"

I still had ten more minutes of freedom. I waited until we were officially open for business before I answered.

Toward the end of the workday, I was playing with my nephews, helping them put together their new Lego sets they got for Christmas.

"Can I get the new bank password?" you texted me.

"You don't need it. It's not like you make mobile deposits."

"I deserve to know the balance."

"Yes, you do. You're on the account. You can check your balance at the bank or at the ATM. Right now I am bonding with my nephews."

"New password?"

No response.

You were outraged.

"You can reschedule the jobs for tomorrow. I have to go to the bank to try and get access to my own bank account. Thanks."

"You have all your clients' contact numbers. You can call them individually and reschedule them yourself. You want me out of the business, run the business yourself."

"Gonna have a lot of unhappy people calling tomorrow, all over a password."

No response.

"The funny part is you probably think I'm bluffing."

No response.

"Don't piss it all away over personal stuff."

No response.

"I don't understand why you're gonna piss it all away? Pretty soon you won't even have to talk to me."

No response.

"I'll take a wild guess and say you're already trying to drain the account and you don't want me to see what you're up to. That sound about right?"

"OMG. You're delusional and pathetic."

"I hate the way you talk to me."

"I hate that I ever fell for your lies. You played me. You used me. You knew exactly what you were doing."

"You're acting like I planned this all out. You know that's not true."

"This is the life you wanted, Thomas. A life with her after I kept her seat warm. You thought I was going to continue to build your empire? She's had your heart since you were sixteen. Even though I was there for you during your sickest and darkest days."

"I understand why you hate me, I do. But it doesn't mean I like it, or I like what I've done. You were perfect in every way. And you're right, what I did was selfish and hurtful. And I will be forever sorry. I never meant to have any of this happen. But it did. And it will ultimately lead you to where you're meant to be. Pretty soon you won't have to talk to me and it will get better. It will get easier. But this business can't work if one of us decides to leave. You know that. We are helping so many people and we are both good at what we do and are the only people who can get the job done right."

"You already made it clear you want me to leave. You will be buying me out. This is not my business for much longer. You're going to be on your own. You should probably tell Whitney to put the papier-mâché and macaroni noodles on the back burner. You want her to run this business? May 13th is the deadline. I'm out."

"I appreciate the heads up."

"I'm a stand up person, Thomas."

"I know."

"So, what, she's going to run the business? Don't expect me to train her how to do the job."

"She's not gonna be doing it."

"Why not?"

"She's not smart enough. You'll train someone else."

I couldn't control my laughter. My nephews looked up from their Legos and smiled, thinking I was happy.

"You expect me to train someone to run a company I will no longer be a part of?"

I know you were shitting yourself because you went quiet. You're scared to be a solo business owner.

Then you had the balls to ask, "Are you sure this is what you want?"

"No, this not what I want! I didn't want any of this! I didn't want to piss away my twenties. I didn't want to fall in love with someone who did nothing but use me. I didn't want to be cheated on and humiliated. I didn't want to start a successful business only to walk away. I am fucking heartbroken, Thomas!"

"I know. It's just that we make a good team."

"I know that, you fucking asshole!"

Dear Thomas,

I received some comical text messages. Someone apparently keyed Whitney's car in Malibu. Several people asked if it was me. Definitely not. Keying someone's car is not my style, but if I ever find out who did, I owe them a high-five.

Since I was playing in the snow the past few days, I needed to catch up on bookkeeping, so I logged into your Amazon account to download any receipts you failed to send, which is typical when you purchase more tools. You bought pepper spray and a taser gun and had them shipped directly to Whitney's address. Is this because someone keyed her car?

Remember when a homeless person let himself into my house back in November 2020? He scared the shit out of me and Alice. Where was *my* pepper spray and taser gun?

You obviously never gave two shits about my safety.

This bitch gets her paint scratched and you're buying her pepper spray? She lives in Los Angeles. Why the fuck wouldn't she already own pepper spray?

Dear Thomas,

The phone rang nonstop today and it was all you.

You called because you needed help putting an invoice together (either incompetent or because you love the sound of my voice, knowing I'd answer); you called to tell me when you were leaving a job site and heading to the next (you don't need to tell me, just change the time stamps in the app); you called freaking out that you didn't have the gate code to a property (the gate code was written in two different places in the client profile); and one of our work vans is currently being rebuilt so you called to ask about the status of the repairs (just call the mechanic directly).

We got a nice review on Yelp. I post all Yelp reviews to our Instagram account, but you blocked the business profile to hide from me. So, I texted you a screenshot of the review with, "I guess I have to text you reviews now since you're the type of loser who blocks their own business IG account. You're welcome for building you a business that people now only go to for their air conditioning maintenance."

"So, you built it by yourself? Wow, thank you so fucking much. Fuck you and your shitty attitude. Have a wonderful day, unless you have other plans. Oh wait! You do have other plans! You decide to be a bitch every day."

"No, I built this business *for you* because you're incapable. My shitty attitude? Have I ever hurt you, Thomas?"

"You say horrible shit to me every day. I'm sick of it."

"Because you're a horrible person. I am sick of your existence. Don't ever call me a bitch, like you don't fucking deserve me not being nice to you. Trust me, you haven't seen me be a bitch yet. You want the real bitch to come out?"

"You're gonna end up getting yourself into a lot of trouble."

"I have not one single reason to be nice to you. You used up all the nice love from me when you rotted in an ICU coma for 23 days, when you were homeless, when you were hungry, when you were locked in jail for 10 months, when you lived in treatment for 24 months, when you moved in with me to a cushy home on Maui. I can't get in trouble, Thomas, I'm smarter than that. But if you want a reason to call me a bitch, I'll give you a reason."

"I have already apologized. I will not be threatened like this."

"Threatened? Fuck you."

"Fuck you too, Danyelle."

Silence for an hour, and then a text:

"I apologize for my temper. But goddamn, Danyelle, back off the nastiness. It's super toxic. I understand you're angry. We're almost done and I'll be out of your life."

"You literally 'apologized' yesterday because you needed me to run your business, not because you were sorry. Stop acting like you don't deserve what I say to you."

"You'll be happy one day, and grateful I left so the right person can love you fully. With their whole heart."

"I will never trust *anyone* enough to let them love me because you fucked that up. You fooled me with your 'infinity love.' Let's be clear. I will not be training anyone to be your next admin person. I did not go into business with you to be a *business* partner. I started this business for you to be your *life* partner. This entire breakup is extremely personal. It was never business."

"Let's just try to act like adults until we get you out and on your way. I think $20K is more than enough for your buyout."

You think I am only worth $20,000?

I have surpassed the point of outrage. Do you know who I haven't spoken to in a while? Whitney. It was time to give her a call.

"It's time to talk again," I said, and she hung up. I sent her a text: "Call me and apologize, woman to woman. You told me you're a compassionate person. After what you've done to me, to another woman, you owe me an apology and an explanation."

"I don't owe you shit, Danyelle. And if you keep harassing me, I'll get a restraining order. You're fucking insane. I did nothing to you. Leave me the fuck alone."

"Harassing you? This is the second time I've *ever* contacted you. First time was four months ago. Don't tell me I am insane. What I did for Thomas is insane. Why weren't you together this entire time? Why did you waste people's time? Why did you hurt other people? You owe me an apology."

"No wonder he broke up with you. He deserves so much better than your psycho bullshit. I don't owe you an apology because I didn't do anything wrong. You're harassing me for no fucking reason."

"So much for being compassionate."

"I get that you're in pain, but I did nothing wrong. For you to keep contacting me is insane behavior."

"I'm asking for an apology. That is not harassment."

"You need professional help. Call a therapist."

"Wow."

While texting her, I received a message from you:

"Stop texting my girlfriend, you fucking psycho!"

"Don't ever call me psycho! And don't ever refer to her as your girlfriend to me."

"You need help."

"I need help? Who's fault is that? Who the fuck was the only person there for you when you needed help?"

"If you try to contact her you will be fucking arrested."

"You two are dramatic as fuck. I cannot be arrested for asking for an apology."

"If you're not in therapy, you need to be. I'm serious."

"Who the fuck are you to tell me I need therapy when you dis on therapy all the time? Thomas, you need fucking therapy. How dare you tell me to get help when you did this to me."

"I seriously want you to get help because I care about you, Danyelle."

"You would have never done any of this if you cared about me. It's like you're holding me underwater and screaming at the top of your lungs, 'I just want you to breathe!' yet you keep pushing me down deeper."

January 14, 2022

Dear Thomas,

I have been off island for over three months and am trying to heal, but as long as I am in communication with you, you keep me from healing. Not only have you hurt me, but you have taken away my healing process since I have to talk to you five days a week for business.

My lawyer ran the numbers for me. I need to know my options. I provided our gross sales for the 2021 fiscal year, and the projected revenue expected, which I could easily double by filling our schedule six months out with repeat customer appointments. He informed me that I was entitled to a payout of more than half a million dollars.

There is no way I am getting that much money from you. You wouldn't be able to pay me that in a couple years and I'm not interested in a ten-year payout, like alimony. If this situation were in reverse, I sure as shit would not pay you that amount. If I had to pay you *any* money, it would happen after a routine drug screening because the second you pissed dirty the payments would terminate.

Before meeting with my lawyer, I ran a background check on Whitney. It's fucking convenient for her to want to be in a relationship with you. Why is that, I wonder? What does she want with the business? Apparently, she filed for bankruptcy in October 2020. *Bankruptcy*. Are you kidding me? I worked my ass off to pay off $38,865.28 of debt. I made sure you and I cash-flowed this business. I was a massive contributor to bringing in almost $400,000 gross in the first ten months of business. And you left me for a bankrupt bitch?

Dear Thomas,

> "An arrow can only be shot by pulling it backward.
> So when life is dragging you back with difficulties,
> it means that it's going to launch you into some-
> thing great. So just focus, and keep aiming."
> – Paulo Coelho

I have always wanted to get a tattoo of a small arrow to remind me of that quote, so I did. I love my arrow tattoo. It's small and dainty and a subtle daily reminder that when life feels this rough, it's time to buckle the fuck up because the universe is about to shoot me forward.

In San Luis Obispo, I went hiking with another friend from college. He said to me, "Whoever your next person or your life partner is, it's not going to be based on infatuation, it's going to be based on timing. It's going to be the right time for you and the right time for them, and you're going to want the same things in life."

"I never thought of it like that. I guess, for me, it was always infatuation."

"And look where that got you."

I needed to see my brother, so I went to dinner with him and his wife. My sister-in-law knew I had been hiding something. I was dreading telling them, but I knew I had to. They were disgusted and hurt for me. She said the weight of my pain made so much more sense to her now. She knew my breakup sucked but thought I would have been feeling better by now, until I let her know exactly what went down. She was livid but supportive in reminding me that I am so much better off without you, and my brother was pissed when I told him how I found out that you drove through Morro Bay.

"If I'd seen him in our town," he said, "he wouldn't be capable of walking or talking right now. But you know what? He will get his karma one day."

"You think so?"

"I know so. He is not going to get away with this."

I cried because I was reminded what it felt like to have the support of my brother and his wife. I cried because I felt stupid I didn't tell them sooner.

Dear Thomas,

The last time I was on island, I was in a terrible place. I was comfortable being around my family and friends on the mainland, and not being in the same state as you. I have stayed in so many different places the past four months, but I am finally coming home.

Kaed picked me up and we immediately hit the food trucks for lunch. On the drive to Lāhainā, I noticed one of the work vans on the highway. Apparently, you let workers drive the company vehicles for personal use on the weekends now.

When I opened the door to my room, I found my cat sleeping in the sun. I buried my face in his neck and gave him kisses while scratching his back. After being gone for over four months, he displayed more affection in that moment than you were ever capable of providing. And, he's a feral asshole, so what does that make you?

I lived in this bedroom for eight months before you moved in. While waiting for you, I had conditioned myself to sleep on my side of the bed, to only use half the closet, and kept your nightstand empty. Waiting for *my* place to become *ours*. Then you broke my heart after marking your territory.

I hated being in this room after you and I shared it. Now that I am back, and so much time has passed since I have seen you in this room, it no longer feels like a space we once shared. It feels like my room again, and only mine.

February 4, 2022

Dear Thomas,

I haven't been back for a full week yet, but I am grateful my friends Bella and Edward are visiting. They keep my mind distracted. Bella and I stayed up late the first night while I caught her up on what happened between us … or should I say what happened between you and Whitney? Bella has a special place in her heart to hate you.

Before we left for whale-watching this morning, I was in the living room with my back to the street. Edward walked in while brushing his teeth.

"Who's in the backyard?" he asked.

"What do you mean?"

"There are two guys dressed in uniforms in the shed."

I slowly turned around and noticed the large utility van blocking the driveway.

"Oh my god," I said, "it's Thomas."

What the fuck are you doing here?

Back in December I told you to take the HVAC shed off my property, and you didn't do that until a couple weeks ago. And you're still storing shit in *my* shed?

I don't want to see you.

I don't want to be seen by you.

I don't want you to know I am back on Maui.

February 7, 2022

Dear Thomas,

Business unfortunately goes on as usual. I still have to answer your redundant calls each day. Today I scheduled an install in Kāʻanapali. I also squeezed in a job at the end of the day—a repair you couldn't get to the other day—and you insisted I schedule it for this evening. It was 4:30 when you called and said you weren't going to make it—the job you insisted I schedule. You had commitments at the AA club. Why would you schedule something else when you already made a previous commitment for your own company?

I don't appreciate you bailing on our customers, especially since you don't have the balls to call them yourself. You always make me communicate the bad news. When our customers aren't happy, I'm the one who gets my ear chewed out, not you.

Bella scheduled a sunset family photoshoot in Kapalua. We left my house and, on the way, saw you driving the work van out of your driveway. The clock read 5:15. You finished the install job before 4:30, which means you had *plenty* of time to go to the next job and still make it to your bullshit commitment at the club. You fucking lied to me, and I caught you.

You have no idea I am on island, and I can see exactly where you are, which is not where you said you were. You are a liar, and a grown man who lies is a fucking weirdo.

Dear Thomas,

My focus this week is therapy. For starters, I went to a Booty Barre class in Pāʻia with my friend Lena, followed by a walk on the beach. While sitting with our toes in the sand watching humpback whales breach, Lena said something no one else has said to me.

"I think what you're going through is fucking shitty. I think the universe is making you go through this so you don't have a shitty life with him later."

It hit hard; so hard, I might just accept it.

I had pictured a perfect life with you, especially since we had survived the darkest days. Our future was going to be smooth sailing. But what if she was right? What if we had stayed together and it turned out to be a shitty life? I proved to the both of us that I was never going to leave you, and by doing that I endured the most painful shit I have ever had to endure, but if leaving saved me from having an even more agonizing life with you, I'll fucking accept that.

I decided it was time to try something I have never done before—reiki therapy. I had my first appointment with Reiki Vee a few days ago. I had no idea what to expect or what I'd get out of it, but I was open to trying anything and everything to heal.

On my way to her house, I noticed traffic backing up on Honoapiʻilani Highway, which usually means either a car accident or a fire. Good thing I wasn't driving that direction.

Reiki Vee started with asking me why I decided to call her to set the appointment. I opened up about our history and what being in love with you has done to me. She inquired about past toxic relationships and I mentioned my dad.

"I am estranged from my father," I told her.

"Where were you in your relationship with Thomas when you ended your relationship with your father?"

"Thomas had been missing for a month," I said and cleared my throat. "The morning after I cut my dad out of my life, Thomas contacted me by phone."

"So, you ended one toxic relationship, making room for another."

I always remembered you resurfacing in my life after that horrible night when I told my dad he was dead to me. I never thought of it as a toxic karmic cycle.

I told her how much I had been vomiting since this betrayal happened.

She reviewed the different chakras and explained, "The gut is the yellow chakra. It represents personal power, and when you felt powerless or the betrayal was out of your control, it resulted in you throwing up 'for no reason.' The throat chakra is blue. It represents communication. You are constantly clearing your throat or coughing because you are not speaking your truth. The energy in your throat chakra isn't moving well."

I was on the table and she had her hands on my temples when I saw the color purple. She was working on my third eye chakra and said, "The word 'rescue' is coming to me. What does the word 'rescue' mean to you?"

"I don't know," I said and shrugged.

"Take your time," she said. "This isn't a test."

I thought about what the word might mean to me.

"Honestly, I have always been the one everyone goes to for rescuing. My coworkers when they needed a shift covered. My friends when they need a babysitter or a ride to work. I've had friends ask to borrow money when I needed money just as badly. I have rescued Thomas the most. I have provided him with money, shelter, food, clean clothes, and I put gas in his truck when he didn't need to drive anywhere. I kept his life manageable. Even after Thomas got sober, I rescued him by answering his phone calls while he was in jail. I sent him clothes when he got to rehab. I rescued his lack of security when he asked me to open a business with him."

"Mm-hmm …"

This is when the epiphany hit me.

"Just because I have never gone to anyone to be rescued doesn't mean I haven't *needed* rescuing. I never asked for help until now. The past four months on the mainland, I surrounded myself with loved ones, and I did something I don't normally do: *I let them rescue me.* I surrendered and accepted the help. I let them open their homes to me, I slept on their couches, or in their spare rooms, and ate their food. I absorbed their advice, love, and support."

I then thought about my biggest rescuers: my roommates. Taya, Kaed, and Mia are angels sent from god. They witnessed me at my lowest, darkest, and most angry moments. They all heard the screaming. Taya and Kaed ran in on me beating the shit out of you, ready to protect me. They held down the fort and took care of my cat, allowing me to go home to be with my family and friends, something *you* refused to do. I'm not sure I can ever express to them how grateful I am. Mia has stayed up with me many late nights. She is kind, gentle, and unbiased. She has helped me see things in a different light. She is well aware I could be one of those Scorpios incapable of forgiveness, because I don't *understand* forgiveness, but she wants me to heal just as badly as I want to heal. She was the first to tell me to leave the business—as soon as you left me—because she hated seeing me torture myself.

"I want you to envision the life you desire for your future," Reiki Vee said.

"A life of peace. I envision boundaries to protect my peace. I picture myself alone because life will be peaceful without someone hurting me."

"Keep going," she said.

"I'm thinking about all the women in my family before me. All the abusive men in my family. All the drugs and alcohol and parties and belittling of women. I'm thinking about how I am going to be the one who breaks the cycle of abused women in my family. I'm thinking about the weight of the responsibility to take on that role."

It's a lot of pressure to be the one to break the cycle. It's an exhausting position to be in, yet inspiring for my future generations.

After the reiki session, I was sitting in my living room taking everything in. Taya asked how it went, and I shared that it was eye-opening and truthfully mind-blowing.

"I'm thankful Thomas still doesn't know I am back on island. I cannot believe he came over here the other day to get stuff out of the shed. Luckily Edward noticed him in the backyard before he saw me."

"Wait, who is in the shed *right now?*"

"What?"

"Someone is in the shed right now."

We looked out the window and there you were, *again*.

Why do you still come to the house? I told you to get your shit off my property months ago! I looked at the clock and it was two in the afternoon.

"What the fuck is he doing here?" I said. "He's supposed to be at an installation job in Kīhei right now."

Maybe you didn't leave Lāhainā in time, I wondered, and the traffic on Honoapi'ilani Highway had you stuck on the west side, but no, I received a bank notification that you paid for the equipment in Kahului. I called our supplier's warehouse there and they confirmed you had picked up the equipment this morning.

So, I did the math and figured it out. You drove to Kahului and sat in traffic for two hours to get something out of my shed, something that *shouldn't* be in my shed to begin with, and something you could have bought at Home Depot while you were already in Kahului. What a waste of gas money, and time. And now you would have to sit in traffic again to drive to the south side. I wanted so badly to walk outside and scare the shit out of you, but I still didn't want you to know I was back. I wanted you to leave me alone and I now have a one-up on you.

I waited twenty minutes and texted you, "Hey, I need the photos of the model numbers and serial numbers for this job so I can register the customer's warranty."

"I'll get it to you soon."

Not a lie, but dancing around it.

I called you a half-hour later.

"How's the install?"

"It's going good," you said, the call breaking up.

"Why can't I hear you."

"'Cause I'm driving on the Pali right now."

"Why are you not at the job site?"

"I had to drive back to Lāhainā. I forgot something."

"That's not a waste of gas money at all."

"Yeah, I make mistakes, Danyelle."

"You sure do make a lot of mistakes."

The call ended.

Today is another day gone and you still don't know I am back on Maui, and it feels good knowing that. You don't need to know I am back on island.

I took the ferry to Lānaʻi to relax at my favorite beach in front of the Four Seasons resort. I hadn't see my friend Lily in a long time. She knows you left me but didn't know the details. Telling Lily everything from the beginning was like beating a dead horse, but it was the first time I told someone without crying. Is this a sign I am getting better? Lily's jokes might have helped. She's a good shit-talker and knows how to put a smile on my face.

It's only been a couple days, but I have noticed the reiki therapy has mellowed me out. Maybe I am starting to heal.

Dear Thomas,

"Do you know what today is?" I texted you.

"No, what?"

"You really don't know what today is?"

"Uh, no I don't."

"Today marks one year of being in business."

"Oh cool!"

"And do you also know how fucked up today is? We should be celebrating $410,400 in our first year! We should be celebrating together as business owners after all our hard work to make this happen. We should be doing something to celebrate and you fucking ruined it."

I have learned that being in business for yourself is a 24/7 job. It never stops. You don't sleep much, worrying. You grind your teeth, stressing. You talk in your sleep, saying things like "accounts receivables / accounts payable." Opening a company from nothing is rewarding yet overwhelming. And working with you, Thomas, is exhausting.

We do not share the same vision of reputation and success, which is why you used me to open this company. If you and I never dated and you came to me asking if I wanted to start a business with you, the answer would have been 'fuck no.' You are dumb and you defend your stupidity. If you are not dumb, then pretending to be is not cute.

You have no idea how tedious bookkeeping is. When you drop off receipts, I have to go through every single one to circle the date, invoice number, amount, and form of payment. Then I organize each in order by date. You write on the gas receipts, "gas." No shit, it's fucking gas, and you fail to specify which vehicle you are refueling.

I scheduled an oil change for the larger utility van and the mechanic noticed a nail in the tire. The tire needed to be replaced, so I called the tire shop and they ordered another that would take a week to get to the island. The next day, you drove that same van over more nails and punctured an additional tire. You called and instructed me to call the tire shop again to have them order a second tire so we could replace two at once, but this second tire was patchable. I don't understand your thought process. The first thing that comes to mind is to call Danyelle? Why wouldn't you man up and think to yourself, *Maybe I should swing by the tire shop during my lunch break and see if it's patchable*. Sure enough, it was. I saved us $500.

When the day came to replace the original tire, the mechanic lost the key to the van. You called asking if I could bring the spare.

"No," I said, "the key is at the auto shop."

"The guy can't find it."

"Well, it's there, so tell him to look for it."

The key was in his back pocket.

On the daily, you call asking questions you don't need me to answer. You ask if certain customers paid their bills. You ask when the van will be out of the shop. And you always love asking for the gate codes to properties, even though every fucking gate code is in the customer's profile in the work app, which is accessible from *your* phone. One time you called because you didn't know how to exit out of a gated community. You wanted me to call the homeowner (who was standing maybe forty feet behind you) to buzz you out. All you had to do was drive six inches forward so the sensor would trigger the gate. And it wasn't just you. You had an employee with you. Two grown men couldn't figure out how to exit a gated community?

You cashed out a job for $171.88 recently but never deposited the cash into the bank account. When I asked you why not, you said, "We don't charge that customer because it's charity and we can write it off for taxes." Then don't 'cash' it out! If you're promoting a charity, add a "promo" line item to the invoice, making the balance zero.

I am practicing emotionally checking out of this business.

"We have to talk about this customer," you texted the other day.

"What is there to talk about?"

"She wants a discount because we finished a day early."

"It's your company, your decision. My opinion and feelings don't matter. What does Whitney think? Since you'll be spending the rest of your life with her, her opinion must matter."

"Just knock off $300."

"Whatever you say, your majesty."

You also piss away money on labor. I found out our employee Oscar went with you to pick up some equipment. Of course, we have to pay him for his time, but why are we paying him to sit in the passenger seat for an hour? He could take the morning off or be doing something productive.

"I'm not gonna cut his hours every chance I get," you said. "I'm gonna keep him happy. He works his ass off every day. The job we are doing right now is because of Oscar. He gets paid barely anything after the taxes he has to put aside."

"$20 an hour isn't enough? What the fuck kind of world are you two living in? You paid him an extra $30 just to ride in the van with you. I'm baffled you asked me the other day if it was time to up his pay to $25 an hour when you both hardly know how to use the app. You're going to run out of money so fucking fast."

"Hope you're having a beautiful day, Danyelle. Keep living a life full of hatred. I hope it works out for you. I hope you find peace."

You lit a fire under my ass after this conversation. I'm sick of seeing HVAC junk around my house. I told you to get everything off the property back in December, and have asked repeatedly if you still had stuff stored at my house. You lie each time and say no, even though you come by often to get equipment out of my shed.

It's time I let you know I am back on Maui.

I went into the shed and pulled everything out. I assembled a pile of crap. I found old rusty evaporator coils and empty refrigerant tanks alongside the house, and your fucking ever-growing collection of work boots in the carport storage closet. I found duct boards, blower motors, a box of tools, and towels you had said were missing. I took a step back to capture a photo of everything, then sent the photo to you, Oscar, your sponsor, the board members of the AA club, and your closest friends.

"IF THOMAS DOESN'T GET THIS SHIT OFF MY FUCKING PROPERTY TODAY, I AM DUMPING IT AT THE CLUB. YOU DON'T GET TO USE ME, CHEAT ON ME, HUMILIATE ME, AND THINK YOU CAN USE MY PROPERTY FOR STORAGE. I GAVE YOU NOTICE BACK IN DECEMBER TO GET YOUR SHIT OFF MY PROPERTY WHILE I WAS STILL OFF ISLAND AND THIS IS WHAT I COME HOME TO?"

Not one person responded.

"I'll be picking it up today," you texted later.

"NO SHIT."

It must be exhausting being you.

Something I have been reluctant to do is to start telling customers I will no longer be a part of this company. It was heartbreaking to come to that decision. I don't want customers begging me to stay.

I opened up to our VIP customers first; they deserve to know that I won't be around to keep the company from falling apart. Everyone I have talked to (and you better believe I explained what you did to me) has been nothing but supportive. They hurt for me and understand I am devastated. They recognize I poured my heart and soul into this business, and held on for as long as I could, for the community.

"Fuck the community!" one of them said, and I needed to hear that. I needed that blessing. It assured me that I am making the right decision.

"One of your friends decided it was a good idea to cause a huge scene at a gas station," you texted me sometime later, "so she could tell me I was a piece of shit."

You *are* a piece of shit, but I didn't respond.

Do you need me to remind you of the scenes you caused at all the gas stations when I didn't want to buy your drunk ass more alcohol? How about the Broadway musical scene when you ran out of heroin?

"You tell your friends to be careful out there," you texted.

Excuse me? Is that a threat?

"It's funny you're telling people you built this company. Fucking hilarious!"

"I never told my friends that. They *watched* me build this company."

"I apologize. I shouldn't have said that. You can tell people whatever you want. Just be careful if you plan on talking bad about the business."

Another threat?

April 4, 2022

Dear Thomas,

The countdown to my exit is ticking down. I have been dreading discussing a buyout contract with you but it needs to happen. I don't want to give you too much time to dick me around, but I also can't give you short notice.

My lawyer typed up the paperwork to propose what you're going to pay me to get out of this business. Is there ever a good time to serve someone papers? I didn't want to give them to you in the morning before starting a four-teen-hour day. I pictured you throwing a fit and threatening me that you'd either no-show or cherry-pick your jobs. I decided to fuck up your weekend instead.

I dropped the yellow folder on the driver seat inside the work van on Friday night. After I got home, I realized it was April Fool's Day, but this was not a joke.

I didn't hear a peep from you all weekend.

You texted me this morning, three days later: "At some point we need to have a reasonable conversation about this contract."

I thought about how my lawyer told me back in January that I was entitled to more than half a million dollars as a payout. Instead, we proposed $175,000 over a ten-year payout. $60,000 of that would go directly into my retirement account, where it would sit untouched for thirty years.

"This is an extremely reasonable contract."

Dear Thomas,

I discovered something interesting in my mailbox: a letter, from you. A four-page apology. I had asked you eight months ago to write a letter in hopes that when I was having episodes of rage, I would have a letter to read to help me better understand why you did this to me. You always said you were too fucking busy. And now you have the audacity to drop off an apology letter three nights before we are supposed to discuss the buyout? This is so inappropriate. You cannot do anything right.

"Dear Danyelle, my heart aches every day because I have caused you an unimaginable amount of pain."

Unless you feel it on my end, you will never understand my pain, my heartache.

"I carry a lot of guilt for my actions, which were mean and unthoughtful."

Your actions were malicious and undeniably careless. Why would you put yourself in a position to be so awful? You made sober decisions to tear me apart.

"The moment I knew I loved you was when you were scrubbing my infections in a motel bathtub."

Yes, I have heard you explain this to Bryan before. I have known that was the moment you decided to marry me. How deceiving of you.

"I did love you at one point, but the man who fell in love with you is a different man."

I am only worthy of your love when you're fucked up?

"The more changes I went through and the more I started to grow and change in sobriety, the more I noticed my feelings for you were dissipating."

A man who has grown, learned, and changed, would never make a sober decision to hurt someone like this.

"I noticed one day when I said 'I love you' that I didn't mean it or feel it."

You remember the exact night you knew you had to marry me, but you can't tell me the exact day you knew you weren't in love with me?

"I continued to lie, hoping my feelings would change. I hoped I'd fall in love with you because of all the hell I put you through, and the fact that you never left me, even when everyone else had. There was even a moment when I said to myself, 'fuck it,' I'll just marry her even if I don't love her because she's so beautiful and amazing and she would make the best wife, and any guy would be crazy to not marry her."

You *are* fucking crazy.

"I followed my heart and called Whitney and lied about it. I never fell out of love with her and knew I never would."

Both you and Whitney are disgraceful. If you have been in love with each other this entire time. Neither of you should have given a moment of your time to anyone else but each other all these years. You have both hurt a lot of fucking people.

"There is nothing you did to make me stop loving you."

Either I did something to make you stop loving me or you were *never* in love with me. You can't say you were in love with me "at one point." How about you admit why you stuck around? You were in love with how easy I made your life, and you fucking used me.

"When we started hooking up, I made it clear I did not want to be in a relationship. And then I relapsed, and everyone left me, except for you. You stayed through years of mayhem and sickness. I honestly felt I owed you the rest of my life."

Damn straight, you did.

"I couldn't lie to myself anymore. Breaking up with you was one of the hardest things I've ever had to do in my life."

Breaking up with me wasn't hard for you. It wasn't hard for you to use me. It wasn't hard for you to go behind my back and have three one-hour conversations with Whitney before you had the balls to tell me you weren't in love with me. It wasn't hard for you to drive through my hometown when I specifically asked you not to. It wasn't hard for you to blast a photo of the two of you all over social media when my friends and family still didn't know you'd left me for her.

"I apologize from the bottom of my heart. I never wanted to hurt you."

Then why did you? It's one thing to break my heart, but everything you did since then were sober, conscious decisions to hurt me. You are a fucking coward.

"I went behind your back and talked to Whitney and started falling back in love with her while we were still engaged with a set wedding date."

That is cheating, Thomas. You were emotionally cheating on me our *entire* relationship. You cheated on me when you called her to make sure she was available and on board with you leaving me. You wanted to make sure you had a relationship lined up before leaving me. If you wanted to be single after breaking up with me, you would have done it years ago. You didn't want to be alone, so you called her to make sure she was committed to you.

"I have been extremely dishonest, selfish, unthoughtful, and disrespectful. I hope you know that I wish I could do it differently."

Then why didn't you? These past eight months, you could have gone about this in a respectful way, not like a teenage boy who couldn't wait to get his dick wet in Malibu.

"I hurt you deeply and you have turned it into rage. I have done the same thing in the past and have tried to convince myself that rage is not the way. It's poisonous and it only brings more pain and sickness."

What normal human *wouldn't* be angry after all this?

"I still care about you. I still pray for you every day. I know you will be okay."

So, that makes everything you've done okay, because one day *I* will be okay? I didn't deserve any of this. You don't get to be the one who tells me I will be okay.

"If I could take your pain, I would."

This pain would make you relapse.

"I want you to be happy, I really do."

I can see the future: I will be happy one day, and you will make sure to selfishly disrupt that happiness. You will always do what you do to get what you want.

April 11, 2022

Dear Thomas,

Four days ago, you asked when would be a good day to talk about the contract. I told you I was available Monday (today), Tuesday (tomorrow), or this Thursday. Then you asked if we could meet at 6:30 pm like you didn't understand. I just told you when I was available.

That same day you let me know you were out of checkbooks and asked several times if Oscar could swing by the house to pick up one before the weekend, which wasn't necessary. You wouldn't need one over the weekend and weren't picking up equipment on Monday, so I let you know I'd bring a full checkbook to our meeting.

I hadn't seen you since before I left for the mainland in October six months ago. I was nervous because trying to reason with you is like arguing with a teenager. I still can't believe you dropped a fucking apology letter in my mailbox days before we were scheduled to meet.

Nice tactic.

I was finishing entering invoices earlier today when I noticed a check had cashed out. A paycheck for Oscar dated the 8th.

"What the fuck?" I texted you. "You wrote Oscar a check and didn't tell me? You said you were out of checks."

"Yeah, I wrote him my last one. He's paid up already."

"Payday is the 10th, not the 8th. And you overpaid him. You're going to lose so much money with all the confusing work you're going to create for your next bookkeeper. You have had over a year of me telling you exactly what needs to be done to keep the books straight. You have zero respect for what goes on in the back office."

I am counting down the days until I don't have to work with you.

Neither of us brought someone to mediate. I already knew the meeting wasn't going to go smoothly so I prepared to record the entire conversation on my phone. You showed up with Panda Express in a paper bag. Did you think this was going to be a quick meeting? You didn't offer to buy me dinner as a business expense, let alone a coffee … when you were the one who decided we would meet at a coffee shop. This was supposed to be the most serious business meeting we'd ever have, and perhaps our last, and you treated it like a drug deal.

"So, you're proposing $175,000."

"Yes, after ten years."

"It's way too expensive. I'm not going to be able to afford that."

"Yes, you can. That's why it's unbelievably reasonable."

"It's too expensive. We've only been open for a year."

"And we made over $400,000 in twelve months."

"I know. Gross. I still have to pay everybody."

"Well, what do you think is an appropriate number, then? I already gave you a great number, but if you don't think it's a great number, tell me what is. When I found out it was supposed to be closer to $600,000, I about shit myself."

"What was supposed to be $600,000?"

"The payout."

"There's no way I would do that."

"I know you wouldn't, which is why I came up with a reasonable number. I also put myself in your position. If I had to pay you $600,000, that would never happen."

"Why can't we do something like that?"

"Like what?"

"Why don't *you* keep the business?"

"I don't *want* the business. I'm not an AC tech and I wouldn't employ you to be my technician. I'm trying to get the fuck away from you. That's the whole point of this meeting. Why would you even come up with that idea?"

"$175,000 is a good deal. I would rather have that than have to pay you out for over ten years and watch most of our profits go to you."

"You can make a lot more if you keep the business open. You saying you don't want the business validates that you used me."

"I did not use you. I still have to pay my employees. It's just not going to work."

"Then give me some numbers. But for you to sit here and say you now want *me* to buy you out is ridiculous."

"$50,000 cash up front," you offered, "which is a lot of money."

"My lawyer suggested $75,000 up front, but I told him that's not happening, so you're welcome."

"Thank you."

"That I am un-fucking-believably fair?"

"I can do $10,000 in six $1,500 monthly payments."

That math does not add up, but okay.

"I can't do anything more than that," you continued. "If you want anything more, I'll have to start over. I would have to file for bankruptcy."

Was that Whitney's bright idea?

"There is no starting over. I helped you bring in almost $400,000 in a year. You currently have $8,500 pending in accounts receivables. You have $35,000 of projected revenue on the calendar, which I will increase to $50,000 before I leave on May 13th. On average every month we bring in $27,000, but in the last thirty days alone we brought in

$48,000. Having money coming in is not going to be an issue. This whole 'I have to start over' thing is bullshit. You have an entire company, you have two vehicles, you have over 300 customers, and you have nothing but a five-star reputation with reviews."

"I know."

"You're not starting over."

"Well, I will start over if the price is over that."

"What do you mean you're gonna start over?"

"I'd have to liquidate and get a new LLC."

"I just told you everything you have, so, what … you're planning to sell both vehicles, all the equipment, the tools?"

"I'm not gonna sell both vehicles. You can have one."

"That's what starting over is. You're saying 'liquidating,' which means everything down to the last screwdriver."

"I'm not getting rid of my tools. I bought those tools."

"And the business paid you back for those tools, so therefore the business owns the tools, not you."

"Have you ever sold used tools?"

"I don't give a fuck about the tools, Thomas."

"No, I'm not selling the tools."

"You don't pick and choose what to liquidate. Liquidating means that you get rid of everything. Why would you start over when you already have appointments six to eight months out. I'll schedule twelve months out if that's what you want."

"I can't pay more than $60,000. It's a lot of money."

"My efforts were astronomical."

"I know, and I'm going to pay you. It's a lot of money."

"We brought in almost $400,000 in twelve months. This is what you wanted. You wanted this business to explode. You would have more money in your account if you'd pay attention to the fucking gas stations you go to and if you wouldn't buy yourself a pair of boots every thirty days."

"So, you're okay with $60,000 total?"

"I deserve more," I said, "but honestly, I'm not interested in you paying me money for years on end. I don't expect you to be *alive* in ten years. I deserve to be compensated for my efforts and the hell you have put me through."

"I am sorry for that."

"I am also not charging you extra for me to train your brother. I'll go to Kaua'i and train him for ten days. I'll make sure the vehicle is registered out of my name and into the business. Did you forget I have that over your head?"

"No, I didn't."

"This is $110,000 less than what I proposed. To be honest, the $500 to my Roth should go up to $18,000."

"I can't."

"You can. Because that would be three years at $500 per month. The $1,500 monthly payments will be over in six months, and then payments would only be $500 a month."

"That's all I can do."

"Are you shutting the business down in eight months? Are you selling everything and moving to Malibu? How can you not afford $500 a month for three years?"

"It's all I can do, Danyelle."

"You're trying to undermine me."

"I'm not trying to undermine you."

"Why is that all you can do? I deserve an explanation."

"Because I need to," you said, followed by a long pause, pondering lies. "I have to take care of my brother, my employees, I have to make payments to you now, and we are trying to go to a legit payroll soon, so things are gonna get a lot more expensive. This is all I can do."

"Why do you think that's all you can do?"

"I went over this with my financial advisor."

"They should probably call me so I can give them accurate numbers."

"No."

"Do they need to talk to my lawyer?"

"No."

"So, this imaginary financial advisor, did they pull these numbers out of their ass without looking at our bank statements, accounts receivables, and projected revenue? I know you can make these payments for several years because I just explained where all the money's coming from."

"I don't want to make that payment for several years. Just because I *can*, doesn't mean I *want* to."

"So, you *can* make this payment."

"No."

"You just admitted you can."

"Why would I want to? It makes no sense. That's a lot of money, Danyelle."

"Yeah, I know it's not a *little* amount of money. But you have caused a *lot* of damage. Should I throw in my therapist invoices?"

"That's personal stuff."

"Who fucking caused that? How much of this is Whitney's idea?"

"She has nothing to do with this."

"Why did you want me to start this business for you?"

"At the time, I thought it was going to be for *us*."

"*At the time?* We were in business for not even four months when you told me you weren't in love with me, and knew you weren't in love with me *before* that. You wasted my fucking time."

"I'm going to pay you for it."

"I'll take this to my lawyer and see how I feel about this. May 13th, I never want to speak to you ever again."

"I understand."

"Nice tactic by the way, dropping off an apology letter two days ago?"

"That has nothing to do with this. That was not a tactic. I just wanted you to know I was sorry. I feel horrible."

"Obviously you don't feel horrible enough."

"Yes, I do. You can't tell me how I feel. I know I could have done things differently and I'm sorry about that."

"Picking a different time to write a heartfelt letter could have been one of those things."

"I know," you said, sitting there like a dog with his tail between his legs. "So, did we agree on $60,000 total?"

"Yeah, I just want to be done with this."

I gathered my purse and stood up to leave when you said, "I pulled money out of the business account to give to you … when this whole thing goes through."

"What do you mean you pulled money out of the business account?"

"I pulled thirty grand out to give to you."

I sat back down and asked, "When?"

"Today, just before we sat down."

"Why would you take out thirty grand cash?"

"I didn't take out cash."

"How did you pull out thirty grand?"

"I put it in my account."

"That is *not* okay."

"It's for you."

"Leave it in the fucking business account! The business account is supposed to write me a cashier's check, or it's supposed to be direct-deposited."

"It can't come through me?"

"No!"

"Why not? It's for you."

"Then why wouldn't you write it in my name right now? If that's for a down payment or a deposit or a hold or whatever, why the fuck would you put it in your name?"

"So I could write you a check."

"Then write me a fucking check or put it back into the business account."

"Alright. I'll have to go get a personal check."

Silence.

"Your logic is insane. You just love fucking me over. Why would you take out thirty grand to put in your personal account?"

"It's yours."

"So why would it go into *your* account first? Put the money back. So fucking sleazy. Who the fuck told you to do that?"

"No one told me to do that."

"Your financial advisor or your girlfriend?"

"Nobody."

"You just came up with the idea to take out $30,000, and god forbid you get mad tonight, or Whitney doesn't give you enough phone sex, or you spend it on heroin or meth. Why the *fuck* would you take out thirty grand and put it in your personal account?"

"To give it to you as a down payment."

"Then write a check in *my* name, not yours."

"I don't have any personal checks on me."

"*Go get one.* I don't have anywhere to be."

"But can we print something that says I gave it to you?"

"Absolutely. I'll have a picture of it. We'll do it together, side by side, holding hands, skipping through the fucking fields like fairies. Of course, I'll write it down. Even if we didn't, it's time-stamped with the exact amount."

"Okay."

"I cannot believe you did that. Your thought process …
I don't know why I was ever in love with you. I thought we
were both decent human beings."

"We are."

"I thought we had the same views on a lot of things."

"It's *your* money, Danyelle. Don't fucking panic. It's *your*
money. It's going to *you*. Why are you panicking?"

You are such a narcissist.

"I'm fucking pissed. I worked my ass off."

"So did I."

"You and I clearly do not have the same vision."

"Yes, we do."

"No. Like when you texted me three weeks ago 'these
gas prices are killing us.' I'm like, no shit. I don't care if gas
is a dollar or six. I'm so particular with how to save money
and how to be careful with everything, and you make fun
of me all the time. You never take me seriously, you don't
respect me, and you think everything I do is a fucking joke."

"I didn't think it's a joke."

"Go get the check."

"We have to get the agreement typed up."

"Then go put the money *back* in the business account.
You're so manipulating and narcissistic to say it's *my* money
yet you put it in *your* account. What, are you buying Whitney
a fucking car or a diamond ring or something?"

"This is just to, just in case—"

"What is just in case?"

"If you went back on your word."

"When the fuck have I ever gone back on *my* word?"

"You haven't. I'm just saying—"

"How many times have you gone back on your word?
Every time you're in jail. Every time you're in rehab. Every
time you wanted another drink."

"A lot."

"Even Christmas, you told me you were going to block my number for two weeks. You went back on your word three fucking days later because you were annoyed you couldn't access the bank account, and you thought I was going to drain the account then, but I didn't."

"You didn't—"

"You have that much distrust in me?"

"Just in case."

"Have I ever lied to you? Have I ever betrayed you?"

"Danyelle, you're super fucking angry. You fucking hate me. How am I not supposed to think you're gonna try to fuck me over?"

"*That's* how you think I would fuck you over? You don't think I'm a decent person? After everything you have done to me, I am still a decent fucking human being. PUT THE MONEY BACK WHERE IT FUCKING BELONGS!"

"As soon as we get the contract, that is your down payment."

"It's one or the other. Either give me the money now and that becomes part of the contract, stating you already gave me the money, or put it back in the business account where it belongs. The last place it belongs is in *your* account."

"Why does it have to be from the business account? Why are you so worried about it? It's *your* money."

"You're a fucking junkie, you've been to jail, I've rescued you *out* of jail just so you could go back *into* jail, and all the hell you put me through …"

"I don't know if you've noticed, but I am not a junkie anymore. Your money is not going anywhere. As soon as the contract is revised, it's yours."

"You are in-*fucking*-sane."

"Call me insane, but I am being safe."

"That is a slap in the face. It is so insulting."

"I am not insulting you."

"You are insulting me to think I would fuck you over."

"Why wouldn't you?"

"I am *not* Whitney. She'll fuck you over when it's convenient for her. You're alive because of me. You have a business because of me. And now you have $30,000 in your account because of me." I started crying. "It is such a slap in the face. You're a horrible person and I do not stoop to your level and fuck you over after everything you've done, and I deserve—"

"I know, that's what scares me."

"You have nothing to be scared about. You are a piece of shit and I am decent fucking human being. I didn't deserve what you did to me. Put the money back in the business account where it belongs! I'll get everything typed up this week, but it is not okay that you did that."

"I might have been a little paranoid."

"When have I ever given you a reason to be paranoid?"

"You haven't, Danyelle. I'm sorry. It's my bad."

"A slap in the fucking face."

"I'm sorry—"

"No, you're not! Every time you say you wish you could do things differently, that you wish you didn't hurt me—"

"I'm just being safe, Danyelle. I grew up poor and never had anything. *Okay?* This is the first time I have ever had something."

"You and me both."

"And I am just trying to protect my share right now."

"You are setup for success. I have reiterated that many times: your customer base, the reputation we have built. You will be okay if you choose to get up and go to work every day. And you won't be poor if you quit buying $150 boots every month. And I am not draining your bank account.

You are compensating me for everything I have done."

"So, let's get this signed tomorrow, at the bank."

"What makes you think I have time to meet you at the bank tomorrow? I am remodeling a house. I am working a job four days a week. And I am running this business. Your schedule is full too, by the way."

"Can you have something setup when I drop off the check at your house, something I can sign in writing and can get a picture of—"

"You can do that too. My lawyer isn't going to have this typed up in the next twelve hours. You can print something and have my roommates sign it as witnesses, or the downstairs tenants, or have the whole fucking neighborhood sign the witness lines if you want."

"Can Kaed and Taya be the witnesses?"

"You can have as many people as you want sign it."

"Kaed and Taya."

"You have until tomorrow to fix this insult. I did not think you could hurt me more. I have never felt so broken."

"So, we both sign the contract tomorrow, and you get $30,000 down?"

"Yes, but you are so out of line. It's supposed to come from the business for tax purposes. The government is going to see that money going into your personal account and flag you. I was supposed to get a cashier's check from the business so I could pay my taxes. You complicate everything. I am a professional, Thomas. I have spent money to do this the correct way. You do understand that you will have to pay taxes on the $30,000 if it goes from the business account directly to you, right? I wouldn't have to pay taxes if you're *personally* gifting me $30,000. Put the money back in the business account."

"Okay, you still want to sign the contract tomorrow?"

"I want you to put the money back in the business account. I have paid my lawyer to draw up paperwork to do this professionally. Do you understand this needs to be notarized? What the fuck was the point in meeting tonight?"

"Let's get this new contract typed up and everything will be paid to you from the business account."

I got up from the table and walked to my car, and you climbed into the work van with your cold Panda Express.

April 12, 2022

Dear Thomas,

I do not take pills. I won't even take ibuprofen. Last night was the first night I took melatonin because I needed something to knock me the fuck out after our meeting.

Mia stayed up with me for several hours last night as I sobbed. I had hit a new low. I still cannot believe you took $30,000 out of the business account because you thought I would leave you with nothing. It was so insulting. If I was going to leave you with nothing, I should have done that a long time ago.

I called my lawyer this morning hysterically crying.

"I just want to be done with this," I told him, and he wanted to fight for me more, but I said, "I'm not the fuck-face whisperer. I just want this to be over."

"Okay, Danyelle, let's be done with this asshole."

You knew what you were doing, Thomas. You went into that meeting with zero intentions of negotiating. You had already made up your mind before we met. You bullied me out of what I deserved. You knew I had no fight left in me, just like I couldn't fight you all those times you had begged for me to go to the store to buy you more alcohol. You caused so much unnecessary stress and anxiety for both of us.

"I won't have to pay taxes 'cause I put it back," you said.

I must have scared the shit out of you.

You silly little boy, the IRS is going to flag you when they see that large amount of money go in and quickly leave your personal account.

A handful of friends knew about our meeting, and I woke up to a bunch of supportive text messages curious how it went. If they only knew …

I didn't have the energy to respond to all, but I did reply to Izzy.

"Hey, if you want to come by, I'll be out front doing yard work, taking out my aggression on the hedges."

"What happened?" she asked when she got there.

"I seriously cannot make this shit up."

I told her everything: how you refused to pay me what I deserve, how you were not listening to the numbers or trying to understand. You went into our meeting with your mind already made up. We had an agreement and then you dropped that $30,000 bomb on me.

If I had to guess, once you realized we had come to a cordial agreement, you thought, *Oh shit, maybe I shouldn't have taken that $30,000*. Saying "I put money aside for you" was your way of covering a mistake. And when I got upset, you had to make it sound like you were doing a good thing.

Izzy was speechless. Something I love about my friendship with her is our mutual understanding of the hatred we both have for you. So many other friends tell me things like, "Don't use the word hate" or "you don't mean that," but Izzy gets it. She and I talk a lot about her horrible ex-husband and how it was a learning experience for her to know she deserved so much better, something I am now in the process of learning myself.

April 28, 2022

Dear Thomas,

It has been two months since my first reiki therapy appointment and I was emotionally due for another. During meditation, Reiki Vee mentioned how everything that goes into my mind, body, and soul is either a debit or a credit.

What I am taking in, is it cleansing or clogging me?

It's a healthy question to stop and ask myself whenever I am unsure of something. Moving forward, and considering my participation in the business, what tasks are necessary and which are extra? Is the music I'm listening to making me happy, relaxed, depressed, or angry? What I scroll through on social media, is it benefiting me or is it garbage?

Being the best version of myself takes constant work. On the regular: drink plenty of water, read ten pages of a positive self-help spiritual book per day, practice minimalism, exercise, schedule therapy, get a pedicure, and a monthly massage. I also need to stop each day and remember to fucking breathe. By working on being the best version of me, one day I will find my person.

Reiki Vee knows how hurt and angry I am about parting ways with the business. It was my baby. I was its mother and part of its birth.

"You should be proud of the business you started," she explained. "You should be happy leaving a business that will continue to run because *you* set it up for success."

I have been fighting with you for an apology and an explanation why you hurt me, but I overlooked what you owe me: a big fat thank you. You should be thanking me for what I built for you. You had said it yourself before we opened: if I wasn't onboard to start this business, you would have never started it. Because of me, you have a successful business.

You do not thank me enough. You do not even realize what you have. You are able to give your brother a job, *my old job*. I created your family business, but you kicked me out of the family.

May 11, 2022

Dear Thomas,

My lawyer typed up the final contract, we had it notarized at the bank, and you signed six months of checks dated and written out to me. Once the first check cleared, I booked a plane ticket to Kaua'i to train your brother. It was bittersweet.

I like your brother and his wife. They have been family to me for a long time. I asked him ahead of time if he would be open to having a heart-to-heart conversation, otherwise my ten days on Kaua'i would have been extremely uncomfortable. Your dad abandoned me, which has taken a toll on another piece of my heart, and I want to hate your entire family, but your brother and his wife weren't a part of this betrayal and honestly had no idea what had happened. They were convinced you had relapsed because there was no way in hell you would have done what you did to me sober.

Your brother is angry with you. He hurts for me. He is mad at you for what you have done, and he is mad at Whitney for hurting you all those years ago and then coming in like a wrecking ball—and causing more pain—because it was a convenient time for her.

I trained him how to manage the company. I introduced him by phone to our suppliers, vendors, contractors, and property managers. We went over manufacturing brands. We went through customer profiles and made notes on equipment, schedule specifications, and our favorite customers and those we dread or flat out refuse to service. We spent several days filling the schedule with service appointments for the next six months on your calendar. I am leaving you with over $50,000 of projected revenue. You're welcome.

All you have to do is get up and go to work. Your brother and I also spent a couple days running errands. We picked up office supplies and added him as an authorized user to the phone and bank accounts.

I brought three hundred farewell cards and handwrote all the customers addresses, which I mailed out from Kaua'i. Hopefully everyone will receive them by May 14th.

> Aloha. I must inform you with a heavy heart that I have permanently stepped away from this LLC effective May 13th, 2022. It has been an overwhelming and rewarding experience co-creating and building this company. I will always be grateful I had the opportunity to be a successful business owner. Every customer, supplier, and subcontractor has been an absolute pleasure to work with. Each of these lasting relationships hold a special place in my heart. Choosing to step away has been a difficult decision for me. I have made sure the operations of the company will continue moving forward. Mahalo for your patience, kind words, feedback, shared reviews, and continuous support. I look forward to crossing paths with you in the future. – Love, Danyelle.

I wanted to make these farewell cards sting and be more of a dig at you, but my lawyer advised me to leave out my emotions and keep it professional.

As I was walking through the airport to fly back to Maui, I felt a sense of relief and freedom that I no longer have the business phone attached to me. It's something I should have done much sooner. Bookkeeping alone is a full-time job. I should have trained your brother sooner and left the phone in Kaua'i while I continued doing the books on

Maui until my exit date. Another lesson I have learned: it's okay to delegate. I don't have to control everything.

It hardly rains in Lāhainā. I loved falling asleep to the sound of the rain in Kaua'i. I cannot wait to be in the rainforest of Costa Rica in two weeks.

Dear Thomas,

I used to count down the days until I could visit you. I used to count down the days until you moved home. And now I have been counting down to this day for the last five months. Friday the 13th, how poetic. Maybe this will be a bad omen for you.

I was buried in so much bookkeeping that I have been stressing the past few months. I spent the last few days finalizing everything, making sure my name is off the LLC license and liability insurance, and transferring the company vehicle out of my name. I feel like I haven't done my absolute best. Maybe it was *my* best because of the circumstances, but it wasn't *the* best. Inventory isn't exactly on point like I would have liked it to be, but regardless, I set you up for success on a brand new laptop. To be a perfectionist is a flaw, my tough, constant battle.

You almost ruined everything (for yourself) when you moved money from the bank account because you were questioning my character. I was angry and insulted, and almost threw everything in the trash, but I needed to hand this business over with all its ducks in a row.

Because I am a professional.

I was upset when the call center fired me back in 2019 because I was escorted out with loose ties. Loose ties drive me insane. While you have the disease of alcoholism, I have the disease of perfectionism. I suffer from it daily and try to manage, but it is endless.

We decided to meet at the gas station at five o'clock so I could hand over all the administration binders to you and answer any last-minute questions.

"I'm sorry about everything, Danyelle," you said. "I never wanted to hurt you. I didn't plan for any of this."

"Yes, you did. You used me. Everyone knows it."

"Believe what you want, but I wanted us to be business partners."

"That is *why* you used me. You would have never had this company if it weren't for me. What did you expect was going to happen? You thought I was going to continue running your company and making your life easier while you made your life with Whitney? Why did you make me do all this if you were just going to kick me to the curb?"

"I make mistakes, Danyelle."

"Is that your copout, because making mistakes is a part of being human? How many mistakes do you need to make before you decide you will no longer fuck people over?"

Before I got into my car, I looked you dead in the eyes and said my final words to you:

"Fuck you."

Dear Thomas,

It took a few days for it to sink in that I don't have the pressure of owning my own company anymore. You went an entire week before texting:

"Missed a call from the bank today, did they call you? They left me a voicemail that something more has to be done but they didn't explain it well. Did they tell you anything?"

You love being dependent on me. You will defend and deny it, yet you still enjoy coming to me for everything. You can't do anything on your own and take pathetic to another level. What's the status on the van repairs? *Call the mechanic, Thomas.* Did they pay their invoice? *Check the bank statements, Thomas.* What's the gate code for this property? *Look in the app, Thomas.* Now you're asking why the bank called? *Call the fucking bank, Thomas.*

So, I ignored your message.

You no longer exist in my world, and in two days I am leaving the country.

My roommates threw me a going-away party. They hired a DJ, setup a taco bar, a game of Cornhole, and rented a dunk tank. We were testing out the dunk tank and forgot to tape a photo of your face on the target. The guest list included my closest friends, former co-workers, and the neighbors. People showered me with travel gifts: blankets, splash-proof bags, and pepper spray. I received handwritten cards wishing me luck, prayers, hopes for healing, and manifesting that I meet a wonderful Costa Rican man.

May 23, 2022

Dear Tom,

Exactly one year ago today, your son asked me to marry him. Imagine someone holding a remote and being able to pause that moment. Imagine the voice of Morgan Freeman narrating: "Before you say yes, exactly one year from today, you will be flying to another country because this asshole is going to destroy your heart." I wouldn't believe it. Pretty far-fetched? A little out there? Dramatic? Or just another you-can't-make-this-shit-up moment in my life?

Now that we know your son was never in love with me, we can look back and recognize the way he asked me to marry him was equivalent to asking me to the prom. Casual enough to change his mind and choose a different date to dance the night away.

I hadn't spoken to you since September, when I called you to let you know I rearranged your son's face with a shoe. You never reached out to me, so I sent you a text in October to live your life like I was dead.

Last night, I was sitting at my gate at LAX waiting to board my flight to Costa Rica when you texted me, "Hi, Dani. It's been too long since I last talked to you. I think you are a great person and I just wanted to let you know that I still care about you, and I hope nothing but the best for you. I'm so sorry about what happened and if I thought there was anything I could do to change things, I would. Take care."

I wasn't going to let you off that easy. I called you.

"Hi, Dani."

"Hi, Tom. You know, you really hurt me by never reaching out to me."

"After that text message about you being dead to the

family, I thought I was respecting your wishes of leaving you alone."

"That's not what I wanted! You had ten weeks to check on me before I sent that text, but you didn't. You were a father to me, and you abandoned me!"

"Thomas is my son, first."

"I know that. I'm not an idiot. You still could have checked on me. You could have texted three simple words like 'are you okay?' but you didn't."

"I know, I'm sorry."

"Are you thrilled to have Whitney as part of the family again, after all the years of you and Barbara telling Thomas to move on and get the fuck over her? I saved his life! You still have a son because of me!"

"I know. What you did was fucking heroic."

"Would she ever do that for him?"

"No, she wouldn't."

"If she ever speaks badly of me, you tell her to shut her fucking mouth and don't ever let her forget that Thomas is alive because of me!"

"I will. I can promise you that."

I wonder if that opportunity will ever present itself. Will you deliver that message to Whitney the way I would? Probably not. If you ever do, I may never know about it.

"Your son fucked me up so bad. There was a day I screamed so loud at him that I ended up vomiting all over myself while driving."

"Oh my god, Dani."

"Yeah. Imagine that. I looked like the fucking heroin addict in this relationship."

"Jesus."

"Do you know how many times I almost drove off the Pali? I was holding tightly onto the steering wheel, debating, telling myself, *I only have to crank this wheel once to launch myself off the cliff*. I was crying with snot running over my lips because I chose life. How would you feel if I went through with killing myself?"

"I don't even want to think about that."

"Well, someone needs to tell your son to stop fucking hurting people! It's not a joke! If I wasn't as strong as I was, and I had killed myself, how would my family charge Thomas with murder when I was the one who committed suicide because of what he did to me? Someone needs to tell him, 'Don't *ever* fucking do this to another human being again! You have the power to kill somebody!'"

Dear Barbara,

Happy birthday! I woke up thinking about you and wondering where I could find a German chocolate cake. I miss you so much. I miss your smile. I miss your cooking. I miss your love. I miss making you laugh. You would be laughing so fucking hard right now.

Can you say, "*Dónde está* crowbar?"

The past week, I have been renting a loft in San José, Costa Rica. I haven't explored much yet because I am a solo female traveler and my Spanish sucks. I have been catching up on sleep and enjoying not being needed. The true adventure I am seeking in Costa Rica starts tomorrow. My driver is picking me up early to take me to my next destination near the Caribbean Sea. I am renting a casita the next four weeks for $285. Yes, that's the price for the entire month. What am I doing still living in Hawai'i?

You would be laughing because in the loft of this place there is a combined washer and dryer unit, but everything is in Spanish. The owner sent a photo of what the selected settings should look like, but only for the washing cycle. I had no idea if my clothes were drying. They were inside for over three hours. When I ended the cycle early, the door wouldn't open and my clothes were stuck inside. I tried unplugging the machine but that didn't unlock the door either. I tried prying open the door, but it was not budging.

I searched online for the user manual in English, but couldn't find anything. After a stressful thirty minutes, I pushed a few buttons trying to restart the cycle when the lock symbol turned off. I pulled on the door and busted it open. I grabbed all my clothes and threw them on the floor.

I wish I could call you.

We could have shared a good laugh.

You're not missing much. Since you passed, your son was in jail for ten months, then finally checked into rehab for two years. He came up with the idea to go into business for himself but knew he couldn't do it successfully without me. You would have been so proud. You would have bragged about us being a 'power couple' to your friends and family.

What's it like up there? Have you seen what your son has done to me? He and Whitney? Where the fuck has she been this entire time?

I know you have just as many questions as me. Are they together because I put Humpty Dumpty Thomas back together again? Is it because you're gone? Is now just a convenient time for her to love your son? You saw how badly she hurt him. You saw how big of a brick wall I had to break through. I was the only one who didn't leave him, and you were the first to point that out. You would say to him all the time, "Don't fuck it up with Dani."

He did. He fucked it up big-time.

Thomas obliterated any chance of us ever being friends. He disrespected the one person who made sure he was okay when no one else did. Good people don't treat people like that. People don't abandon who they love, they abandon who they use. He fucking used me.

I know it hurts you to see me hurt. I know you rooted for me. I know how much you loved me because you told me all the time. And you loved how much I loved your son.

Can you believe Whitney tried to tell me that she and Thomas never actually broke up? She wasn't there for him during his darkest days; she wasn't even sure if he was alive. Who is she trying to fool? If you were here, you'd slap the bitch for saying such a thing. She has hurt a lot of people from being so selfish. Both of them have.

When Tom offered your son your gold wedding ring to propose to me, Thomas respectfully declined for a couple reasons: I wear silver, not gold, but the real reason is that he was never in love with me.

I have to be firm when I say to you, Barbara, I promise I will never do anything for your son ever again. I will never rescue him, never save him, never help him, or do anything that will ever benefit him. I wouldn't even give him the bananas I pick off my açai bowls if he were starving on the streets. He is not my problem anymore.

For the first time in his thirty-seven years of life, he no longer has you or me to run to when shit hits the fan, because we are both dead to him. He can no longer call, no longer has access to our money, and he can no longer come to us for advice or for any kind of love.

Thomas is completely on his own now. He thinks he has grown but let's see how he handles himself when that atomic bomb of karma drops on his ass.

I love you, Barbara. I will see you again one day, but I know you will see your son before you see me.

Dear Thomas,

I am on a boat in the middle of Bocas del Toro as I write this. The best part is that you have no idea where I am; one, because *no one* knows where I am, and two, because you wouldn't even know where to find this place on a map.

I have been having the time of my life in Costa Rica, and now I am in a different country. I hopped on a bus with cool people I met and we crossed the border to Panama. We are renting a bungalow on the water on a tiny island, which is a dollar water-taxi ride from the bigger island. We hired local guys to take us around the small islands of the Caribbean. We bought them lunch, a case of beer, and paid them a couple hundred bucks to be our private tour guides. I am soaking this all in. I am supposed to be right here, right now.

Random thoughts hit me at random times, and I just had an epiphany: if I were to meet a girl going through what I had gone through, what would my advice to her be?

"Walk away," I would say. "Walk away and never turn back. Leave him. This is his story, not yours. This is not your purpose. You are way too beautiful and smart and talented to be wasting a minute of your life on him. You were not put on this planet to take care of this motherfucker. You are working way too hard to barely keep your head above water while all he does is tie weights to your ankles."

This would be my advice.

"And when I say *walk away*," I would tell her, "I mean *stay the fuck away*. Don't go back to him. Don't even consider giving him another chance in the future after he gets sober on his own. This will always be a part of his life and it will never get better."

I would tell her to not be like Whitney. "Either commit to staying or leave forever." I would tell her, "An addict will rearrange their bullshit to make it look like they have changed, but a tiger never changes his stripes."

Dear Thomas,

I spent the past five weeks traveling through Central America. I have met amazing people along the way. I have eaten at some of the nicest restaurants for the cost of eating from a food truck in Maui. Every night I fell asleep to the sound of the rain, and every morning woke to the sound of howler monkeys and birdsong. I am sad this trip is at an end.

"How do you feel?" Xavier texted me while I was at the airport. A thoughtful question.

What did I get out of this journey?

"I forgive myself," I texted back.

Yes, I forgive myself for allowing everything to happen to me. I forgive myself for putting myself through everything I went though. I don't forgive you, Thomas. You don't deserve forgiveness. But *I* do.

I deserve to speak my truths. I deserve to travel. I deserve to be happy. I deserve to love. I deserve an explanation. I also *don't* deserve a lot of things. I don't deserve to be humiliated. I don't deserve to be lied to, cheated on, or deceived. I don't deserve to miss opportunities.

Dear Thomas,

I am sitting around the firepit in my backyard burning relics from the past. I am burning photos of you, and us, jewelry you gifted me, and anything that makes me think of you.

Tonight marks one year since I was blindsided, the day the rest of my life changed forever. I had my entire life planned—career, house, when to get pregnant, who I was going to spend the rest of my life with, and even had the wedding date set—but you had other plans. One year ago, I wasn't sitting in front of a cozy firepit. No, I was in absolute shock.

"I'm not in love with you," you had said.

As everything burns, I can't help but think about the emotional torture you put me through this past year, the humiliation, the betrayal. I hid in the dark, screened phone calls, disappeared from social life, and didn't even pretend to 'fake it' because I didn't care to 'make it.' I had never felt so low in my life. I was unrecognizable by family and friends.

Moving on from you and from this life is the hardest thing I have ever done. I am the only one who knows how much you hurt me. You killed my trust. You changed me.

My heart had to break to clear my vision.

I read an article titled, "We Only Fall in Love with Three People in Our Lifetime" and each love is for a specific reason. The first love is the love that *looks* right. This is the high school sweetheart, a fairy tale, or a country music video. We believe this will be our only love, and we will sacrifice self-growth to make sure this love lasts forever because we are brainwashed to believe it is what love is supposed to be. It's the relationship that appeases our family, friends, community, and society.

I know without a doubt who my first love was. He was my high school sweetheart. The chemistry was fire. It blinded me from the different cloths from which we were cut. I had goals and dreams and plans and calendars. He was content going with the flow and living a one-way ticket lifestyle. I was devastated when he left me, but I moved forward. I have not seen this person in a long time. I imagine if we were to get together again, it would be easy to pick up where we left off because we have done it before. However, I know we could never be together again because he would leave, just like Whitney has done to you. You keep going back to your high school sweetheart, your first love. You like feeling sixteen years old.

The second love is the *hard* love, the love that hurts. There are lies and there is manipulation. We hang on, never letting go. It's a vicious cycle, one we repeat in hopes the ending will be different, but it ends worse than before. It's unhealthy, unbalanced, and even narcissistic. There is emotional and mental abuse. There are extremely high levels of drama. And it's addictive. Like a junkie trying to get a fix, we stick through the lows with the expectations of the highs. This second love teaches us the hardest lessons about who we are, what we want, and how we need to be loved. We think we are making different choices than our first love, but we're not. We are still making choices out of the need to learn lessons. The end goal to make this relationship work becomes more important than the relationship itself, and you will do anything and everything to not hear the words "I told you so." It's the love we wished was right when it's so fucking wrong.

It's easy to point out you were my second love. I did

what I had to do to selfishly keep you alive so I could feel love. I was sucked into the chaos and you controlled the momentum. You were manipulative and deceitful. I thought we were on this rollercoaster together, and I committed to riding by your side. I wasn't going to leave until you cut my restraint and launched me off the track, which you did, leaving me battered and bruised.

Finally, the third love is the love that *lasts*, the love that usually looks wrong yet destroys any preconceived notions of what we thought was love. We finally realize what love is supposed to be. It comes so easy that it doesn't seem possible. The connection cannot be explained and so it knocks us off our feet because we never see it coming. It smacks us in the face. We never plan for it, and we even try to avoid it, but it keeps knocking on the door. It's the love that *feels* right. You come together and you just fit. It is easy, there is no pressure, and there are no expectations. With this third love, you are accepted for who the fuck you are.

I had accepted you wholeheartedly, but I was never good enough for you.

My friends keep telling me I will eventually meet my person, my number three. I roll my eyes because I am done with love and relationships and investing my heart and soul into another person. There are plenty of fish in the sea, but there's also a lot of plastic trash, shipwrecks, whale semen, and chum. They say I will eventually meet 'the one,' and it will happen when I least expect it. Well, then, how the fuck will I know when it happens?

Apparently, I needed to learn what love *isn't* before I can experience what love *is*. I thought I knew what love was until you destroyed me. You will never meet someone who loves you more than I did. You will never experience all three loves in this lifetime.

While our pictures turn to ash, I'm thinking about the love I supposedly won't see coming. I'll look without looking. The possibility of finding my third love is what makes trying again worthwhile. I am certainly in no rush to fall in love again. Falling in love can be scary, especially after what you've done to me, but I know one thing for certain: I will never feel this pain again because no one can ever hurt me like you.

Just because you are sober now doesn't mean you have become a better person than who you were when you were using drugs and alcohol.

I have been working on becoming a better version of myself. I checked off many different forms of therapy this year: running away, couch-surfing from North Carolina to Colorado and all up and down California, my friends and family lending me their ears, listening to tarot card readers, aligning my chakras, writing poetry, recording a song in my friend's basement, and finally writing about all those wild stories to share with the world.

I came up with the idea for writing a book almost five years ago—the last weekend I saw your mom alive, the weekend before I flew you to O'ahu to check you into rehab. I had posted on social media:

Growing up, you are told to stay away from drugs. You are told why they are bad. What you are never told is the hell you will go through loving someone who is addicted to drugs. You are never given a textbook about addiction. You are never given homework on how to handle manipulation and lies. You are never quizzed how to slow the anxiety, how to go with gut instinct, or how to not obsess over what they are doing at all times. It is never explained that you will become a slave to the addict, a detective, a babysitter who has to know their location at all times—what they are doing, who they are with. It is never explained that even if they get through recovery, they are never cured of their addiction; they come back and haunt, turning your perfect world upside-down all over again …

The feedback was overwhelming. I realized I had a lot more friends and acquaintances who related to what I was going through, and I needed to share my story, *for them*. I needed to let any loved one of an addict know they are not alone. I needed to say to them, "I relate to you, and you will be okay."

I am a strong believer that everything must happen for a reason.

Writing a book is possibly the craziest reason why all this had to happen to me. Writing a book has been therapeutic as fuck. After all, someone I trust wholeheartedly once told me, "If reading a book is inhaling, then writing a book is exhaling."

To my family on Maui and across the mainland: You know who you are and what you have done for me. Thank you for picking me up when I fell so fucking hard. Thank you for the sofas, air mattresses, free meals, patience, memories, and the hard lessons. Thank you for believing in me.

To my roommates (Kaed, Taya, Mia, and Anthony): You witnessed my lowest lows. You had to listen to the screams and cries down the hall and through the walls. You held me, fed me, and ran your fingers through my hair. You took care of my fur baby and maintained the property so I could escape for many months. I feel indebted to you forever.

To my therapists (Reiki Vee, several tarot card readers, my kickboxing trainer, hairstylist, and all the ladies who would go hiking with me on a regular basis): Thank you for the long walks, longer talks, the hugs, Kleenex, belly laughs, milkshakes, and what-in-the-actual-fuck screams!

To my lawyer: You are a badass. Thank you for wanting to fight for me even after I threw in the towel, because I am not the fuckface whisperer. Save your energy for my future problems.

To my editor: This book would not be anywhere near what it is without you. You helped make this happen. You watched tears fall onto the pages and felt the pressure I put on myself to meet deadlines I set. You sacrificed your personal time to help make this dream come true.

To my Costa Rica family: I was not expecting you, nor was I looking for you to come into my life. You are the family who brought this book together. Thank you for holding me accountable to my daily goals when it came to writing and reliving this emotional journey. Thank you for the epic memories we created in Puerto Viejo and Bocas del Toro. *Pura vida!*

To Gabriella: Thank you for putting everything in perspective for me. I did not fail as a business owner. I did not sign up for what happened.

To my former air conditioning customers: Thank you for respecting me and giving me your blessings to move on. I provided the community with a wonderful service, but I was my own emergency. As graciously as possible: fuck the community; I needed to serve myself.

To Thomas's family: I promise I will never do anything for him ever again; he's all yours.

And lastly, to Thomas: Fuck you.

I relate to you, and you will be okay.

Danyelle Cedar can be reached at:
dearthomasthebook@gmail.com

@DEARTHOMASTHEBOOK

If you or someone you know has a problem
with substance abuse, find help at:

aa.org
na.org

If you are a loved one of someone with a
substance abuse problem, find help at:

al-anon.org